HANDBOOK

7/83

Handbook of
Western Civilization:
Beginnings to 1700

SECOND EDITION

by Sidney A. Burrell

Boston University

JOHN WILEY & SONS, INC.

New York · London · Sydney · Toronto

Portions of this book are revised and adapted from
ESSENTIALS OF WESTERN CIVILIZATION: THE MAIN STRANDS
OF DEVELOPMENT FROM THE BEGINNINGS TO THE
18TH CENTURY, © 1959 by Howard Chandler, Publisher

ISBN 0-471-12515-6

Library of Congress Catalog Card Number: 76-37642
Printed in the United States of America

Preface

This preface contains some useful study suggestions. Be sure to read it before you go on with the book!

The intention of this book is to give you more than just an outline of historical facts. It also gives you a summary of the major movements and ideas in Western civilization into which the facts can be fitted. This summary and framework will help you to answer essay questions as well as factual and objective questions in examinations.

To make it easier for you to study, the chapters are divided into sections that make it possible to approach the understanding of Western civilization one step at a time. If you proceed with your reading in the following way, you should find it fairly easy to absorb the subject matter.

First: Read Chapter 1, *Western Civilization.* It introduces the main developments or themes stressed in this book. Then read Chapter 10, *The Western World in 1700.* It is a summation of Chapters 2-9, and much that is in these chapters will make more sense to you if you have first read Chapters 1 and 10.

Next: Read Chapters 2-9. Notice that each of these chapters has two kinds of reading matter that cover the same historic topics but in different ways. The first kind (The Essential Movement, white pages) explains the main movements of a convenient chunk of history. The second kind (Events and Definitions, gray pages) gives an outline of facts and additional explanatory material for the same chunk of history. If you read these parts in their order, you will avoid the problem of trying to absorb too much unfamiliar historical detail before you know what a chunk of history is all about. Thus you can obtain a firm and confident feel of the historical period.

Often: Check your memory for ideas and factual details by referring to the brief chronological chart that follows this preface.

Finally: Read Chapter 10; and if you think it may help, read Chapter 1 again.

If you follow this plan carefully, step by step, you will find that you have come to a clear understanding of the development of Western civilization and a sound grasp of factual details.

The Periods of History: Beginnings to 1700

Period of Time	Political Developments	Social Life and Urbanization	Science and Technology	Intellectual Developments
Paleolithic Period (Old Stone Age), to ca. 12,000 B.C.	Family, clan, or tribal organization.	Probably little or no village organization.	Age of food gathering. Tools made of bone, stone, or wood; use of fire by occidental peoples.	Little or no systematized thought; cave drawings.
Mesolithic Period (Middle Stone Age), ca. 12,000–ca. 8000 B.C.	Family, clan, tribe; probably some village organization.	Villages.	Dog domesticated; bow and arrow used.	Probably no systematized thought.
Neolithic Period (New Stone Age), ca. 8000–5000 B.C. Major revolution in human development.	Family, clan, tribe.	Villages.	First use of agriculture (food growing), domestic animals, polished tools. "Neolithic Revolution."	Probably no systematized thought; primitive art forms.
Chalcolithic Period (Copper and Stone Age), ca. 5000–ca. 3500 B.C.	Family, clan, tribe; possibly primitive kingship.	Transition from village to city.	Period of transition when metalworking became common.	Probably no systematized thought.

Period of Time	Political Developments	Social Life and Urbanization	Science and Technology	Intellectual Developments
Bronze Age, after ca. 3500 B.C. Iron Age, after ca. 1800 B.C.	Rise of city-states and territorial kingdoms: formation of Mesopotamian city-states; union of Upper and Lower Egypt, ca. 3200.	Beginning of urban life ("urban revolution"), ca. 3000; rise of commercial exchange; extension of communication.	Use of copper and tin to make bronze; introduction of iron marked last major step in development of metallurgy.	Formulation of mathematics; early astronomy; codes of law; religious rituals and ethics codified; writing developed.
The Ancient Empires to 600 B.C.	Evolution of the divine kingship of Pharaoh; formation of extended territorial empires (Akkadians, Cretans, Babylonians, Hittites, Assyrians, Egyptians). Persian Empire emerges (ca. 600) as greatest united empire of the ancient world before Rome.	Large cities appear; commerce enlarged and extended.	Development of navigation and shipbuilding; applied mathematics; early astronomical calculations.	Evolution of highly developed religious systems: cult of Ikhnaton in Egypt; Hebrew prophets; Zoroastrianism. Development of alphabet; slow spread of literacy.
Hellenic Age, ca. 600–300 B.C.	"Universal" empire of Persia extended its sway throughout the eastern	Continued expansion of city and commercial life; great age of Athens	Formulation of Pythagorean geometry. Sixth century Greeks observe	Greeks develop first true school of philosophy (Milesians), sixth cen-

	Mediterranean; rise of the Greek city-state (*polis*). Persian Empire defeated by Greeks (490–479); conquered by Alexander the Great, 330.	under Pericles, fifth century.	and speculate on the order of nature.	tury. Golden age of philosophy, fifth and fourth centuries: Socrates, Plato, Aristotle.
Hellenistic Period, ca. 300–30 B.C.	Universal empire of Alexander disintegrated into smaller despotic monarchies; Carthaginian Empire destroyed by the rising Roman republic; expansion of Rome.	Growth of commerce and wealth; high level of urban civilization. End of the Greek city-states. Period of great material advance.	Great scientific and technological advances: Euclid (geometry), ca. 300 B.C.; Archimedes (physics), third century B.C.	Hellenic culture spread to all parts of Mediterranean world. Philosophy (Epicureanism, Stoicism, skepticism) partially displaced religious belief.
Roman Empire, ca. 30 B.C.–A.D. 500	Rome became Empire under Augustus, 23 B.C. Mediterranean world unified; Rome reached greatest territorial extent, A.D. 117. Empire Christianized under Constantine, 337. End of Western Roman Empire, 476. Romans achieve high level of government organization and centralization.	Under Roman protection (*Pax Romana*) city life and commerce increased. Economic life of Mediterranean centered on Rome, which had a population of about one million at its height.	Romans reach a high level of practical engineering: road-building, ship construction, aqueducts. No great theoretical advances in science.	Hellenistic philosophies and eastern religious cults gradually superseded by Christianity. Christian theology formulated by the early fathers (Augustine et al.) and partly fused with Greek philosophy.

The Periods of History: Beginnings to 1700 (cont.)

Period of Time	Political Developments	Social Life and Urbanization	Science and Technology	Intellectual Developments
Early Medieval Europe, ca. 500–A.D. 1000.	Centralized Roman imperial government gave way to Germanic successor states. Localized feudal government supplanted Roman bureaucracy. Attempt to revive Western Empire under Charlemagne (800) failed.	Rise of manorialism; decline of city life in northern and western Europe.	Except in Byzantium and Arab world, knowledge was attenuated. Classical influences restricted to narrow elite.	Spread of Christianity; rise of monasticism in the West. Carolingian Renaissance, eighth century.
High Middle Ages, ca. 1000–1400.	Revival of the imperial idea: Holy Roman Empire founded, tenth century. Rise of medieval papacy: Gregory VII (1073–1085), Innocent III (1198–1216), Boniface VIII (1294–1303). Papal decline began with Great Schism, 1378–1417. Growth of feudal kingship marked beginning of national state. Crusad-	Growth of medieval towns after 1000; increase in commerce and wealth; undermining of feudal agrarian society by towns; contraction of European life in fourteenth century; economic and demographic decline until after 1400.	Gradual improvement in agricultural techniques; growing commercial and productive specialization; beginning of large-scale textile manufacture in Flanders and Italy.	Renaissance of the twelfth century; Anselm, Abelard; spread of Aristotle's writings through western Europe. Founding of universities at Bologna, Paris, Oxford, Cambridge. Growth of scholasticism: St. Thomas Aquinas (1225–1274).

Period of Time	Political Developments	Social Life and Urbanization	Science and Technology	Intellectual Developments
	ing movements in Palestine (1099–1204), Spain, and the Baltic region.			
Renaissance and Reformation, ca. 1400–1600.	Appearance of new centralized monarchies; decline of feudal nobility. England, France, Spain emerged as strongest states of western Europe. Beginning of great discoveries: da Gama, Columbus, Magellan. Luther began Protestant revolt against medieval church, 1517. Spread of Protestantism: Sweden (1527), England (1534), Denmark (1536), Geneva (under Calvin, 1540), Scotland (1560), Netherlands (revolt against Spain began, 1567). Counterreformation: founding of Jesuits, 1540; Council of Trent, 1545–1563. Emergence of Spain as leading European power, 1559.	Rich city civilizations in Italy and Flanders. New business techniques ("rise of the capitalist spirit") stimulated commerce. Appearance of commercial financiers: Medici, Fuggers. Price revolution increases European cost of living.	European invention of printing with moveable metal types, ca. 1440. Improvements in manufacture: first "industrial revolution," ca. 1540–1640. Copernicus's *De Revolutionibus*, 1543. Improvements in navigation and shipbuilding.	Thinkers of the Renaissance (Petrarch, Machiavelli) reacted against scholasticism; growing interest in classical literature; shift in outlook from otherworldliness to things of this world (humanism). Protestant leaders reject sacramental views of medieval church; stress faith against works.

Period of Time	Political Developments	Social Life and Urbanization	Science and Technology	Intellectual Developments
Age of Absolutism, ca. 1600–1700.	Development of strong monarchy in France: Richelieu, Mazarin, Louis XIV. Puritan revolution in England (1642–1649); Glorious Revolution, 1688. Beginning of Prussian state under Great Elector, 1640–1688. Westernization of Russia by Peter the Great. Emergence of France as strongest state of western Europe, 1659.	Cities increase in size: London and Paris with half a million people each become largest in Europe. Commercial revolution stimulates capital growth throughout Europe. High point of the mercantile system.	Scientific revolution: change in man's outlook toward universe. Galileo (1564–1642); Newton (1642–1727).	Impact of the scientific revolution felt in philosophy; rise of rationalism. Age of the Baroque in art and architecture.
The Western World, 1700–1789 (Enlightenment and the Old Regime).	Divine right theory of monarchy superseded by "enlightened despotism." Emergence of Prussia and Russia as major European powers. England became leading maritime power after Peace of Utrecht, 1713. Overseas expansion accelerated; Anglo-French colonial wars, 1689–1783. American Revolution, 1776–1783.	Steady rise in European population. Capital growth speeded industrialization in western Europe. Rising social criticism in France.	Newton's discoveries stimulated growth of theoretical science; laws of nature regarded as finally ascertainable by science. Major advances in chemistry, astronomy, biology. Increase in rate of invention (Watt's steam engine, etc.) after 1750.	Newtonian synthesis led to belief in mechanical universe: all knowledge explainable in terms of "natural law"; rise of the "social sciences"; influence of the French philosophes; enlightened individualism and theory of progress dominate philosophy.

Contents

xiv   Contents

chapter eight   *The Age of the Absolute Monarchies*   129

chapter nine   *The Scientific Revolution and the Age
of Enlightenment*   169

chapter ten   *The Western World in 1700: A Summary and Conclusion*   169

Index   189

HANDBOOK OF WESTERN CIVILIZATION: BEGINNINGS TO 1700

chapter one

Western Civilization: Its Components and Its Themes

THE ESSENTIAL MOVEMENT

For the past 200 years the community of European peoples and their offshoots who have settled beyond the seas has been known as "Western civilization." The terms "West" and "western" as applied to the countries of Europe are very much older than that, however, and reach back into the European past as far as the division of the Roman Empire into eastern and western administrative units by Emperor Diocletian at the end of the third century after Christ. The idea that Europe was the "West," as opposed to the "East" of Asia Minor or the farthest Orient, stemmed from a geographical reality that was so plain as to scarcely need explanation: Simply, the region we have known as "Europe" over many centuries is the farthest northwestward projection of the great Eurasian land mass—beyond which, in popular lore, there was nothing but the endless reaches of the "western" or Atlantic Ocean.

In more recent times, but particularly in the nineteenth and twentieth centuries, the term "West" has frequently been employed to designate those nations and peoples, in or out of Europe, whose life styles and levels of material well-being approximated those of western Europe. These have customarily included European nations and nations largely European in origin—as, for example, the United States, Canada, the various English-speaking communities of the former British Commonwealth, and the more advanced countries of the Latin American world. Thus customarily we have come to think of the community of Western civilization as composed of the more "advanced" or "developed" countries, although this definition becomes increasingly less satisfactory as nonwestern countries like Japan move into the category of developed societies.

From a global point of view the definition of Western civilization as a European phenomenon is an exceedingly narrow one, but there is some valid historical justification for it. The Atlantic community (comprising the regions of western Europe and the most advanced countries of the Western Hemisphere) is and has been for a very long time the world's most important development area. While other regions may in time challenge the superiority of this Atlantic region in its areas of greatest achievement—science and technology—the fact remains that this region during the past 500 years has provided a kind of model for the rest of the world's peoples in certain unique ways. For one, it has furnished its peoples with a relatively higher standard of subsistence than the world has ever seen before. In achieving this standard, the region developed skills and techniques for the transformation of natural resources into foodstuffs and manufactured products, which, when applied to military ends, gave the Atlantic countries a long period of economic and often political dominance over non-European peoples. To effect this dominance, Europeans had to move outward across the oceans, a migration that demanded a relatively sophisticated technology. Movement by sea, unlike travel on land, requires specialized knowledge, including shipbuilding and supporting skills such as navigation and pilotage and the ability to load and unload expeditiously while making maximum use of space, as well as an accumulated knowledge of remote lands and peoples. Thus Europe, in order to break the oceanic barrier that surrounded it on three sides, had to reach new levels of organization to develop the skills necessary to the expansion of the European community.

European society began to expand overseas at a time when certain European techniques and skills were just beginning to develop sufficiently to give Europeans a distinct power advantage in their dealings with less developed peoples. Thus the Europeans frequently followed the line of the least resistance and robbed, looted, or conquered peoples whose lack of military and social expertise put them at a disadvantage in resisting European aggression. Here we must have a care before we come too quickly to the value judgment so widespread in our own time among people who sympathize with the historic plight of the non-European peoples who fell victim to European conquest or exploitation. The European conqueror was not necessarily more aggressive, cruel, or immoral than other conquering peoples were. Because of the often superior technical and military knowledge available to him his opportunities to exercise his selfishness were unique, and he took an almost unconscious advantage of those he conquered. There cannot be any justification for the often ruthless manner with which the European treated hapless peoples who stood in the way of his aggressive ambitions. The treatment of the North American Indian, for example, was ruthless, for he was frequently treated as though he did not exist or had no right to exist; as though the vast continent that he and his forebears had inhabited for centuries before the coming of the white European was simply empty land for the taking.

The centuries-old unconcern of the European empire-builder or settler for those whose territories, goods, or natural resources he appropriated has resulted in contemporary antipathy toward the European and all his ways among some of the world's peoples. This is perhaps an extreme way of putting the matter, but throughout the vast regions of the earth known as the "Third World" this attitude toward European and western history is widely shared. The "Third World" comprises a large majority of the human race—all the millions of people who are not aligned with one of two other "worlds": (1) the United States and its allies and (2) the Soviet Union and its allies. In short, the term "Third World" is now used to describe the undeveloped, non-European regions of the world, most of whose peoples have at one time or another felt the economic and/or political weight of western domination.

As a consequence of this widespread antipathy toward Europe and the European tradition, a feeling has grown up both in and out of the Third World that the history of Western civilization is something that must be ignored. For a number of reasons this attitude, while understandable, has shortcomings that in the long run could have adverse consequences for the Third World's future. First, it is never well to ignore knowledge of any aspect of human experience simply because it is unpleasant. The more man knows about himself in every facet of his experience, both good and bad, the more he can hope to reshape the future. Unless we examine the past with an open mind and use historical truth as a foundation for building a better world, we shall find ourselves caught in a swirl of myths about the human condition, which could quickly and surely lead us to destruction.

There are, however, other important reasons for understanding something of the history of the western community of peoples. Western civilization is unique and has played so important a role in world history that to ignore it is to ignore one of the extraordinary developments in the long history of mankind. This viewpoint does not necessarily imply that there is something "superior" about this quality of uniqueness, for the role of Europe in the world historical process is a result of such a combination of causes that we cannot be sure how many of them were the consequences of any innate social or other "superiority" in Europeans and how many were the result of pure chance. No reputable historian, apart from a few intense Nordic supremacists, nineteenth-century white racists, or European nationalists, has ever seriously argued in favor of explicit European superiority over the other peoples of the earth. What most historians have been concerned with is how certain ways of thought and action that developed only in Europe during the past few centuries were able to give to Europe and the whole of Western civilization certain very distinct technological and industrial advantages, which enormously augmented the military and economic capacities of some European nations, so that from the eighteenth through the twentieth centuries they were able to enjoy a kind of global dominance. In addition to military power, western technology and industry helped to raise the mass subsistence levels or standards of living in most western societies to levels unheard of before the twentieth century. At this time such a statement sounds preposterous to some people, for in most modern societies there are many people whose living standards are far below anything like abundance. Many of us are also aware of the tremendous discrepancies between rich and poor, even in the most advanced societies. Nevertheless, it remains true that the West enjoys a greater material abundance spread more widely among a larger number of people than at any other period of history or in any other geographical region.

Even so, many people do not like the assertion that the West has given to its peoples a higher level of subsistence than any other region or community in the world's history. Ideological opponents of capitalism deny the very notion that liberal western societies with diverse ethnic, political, and religious structures have higher standards of living than the "socialist democracies" in other parts of the world, whose mass goals are regarded as purer and more humanistically oriented than those of so-called capitalist democracies. Intentions, however, have nothing to do with the reality of actual accomplishment; despite the questionable merit of the means by which wealth is distributed within a "capitalist" society, it is an indisputable fact that the productive abilities of western countries are far higher than they are anywhere else.

The historian's attempts to explain this phenomenon lie at the base of every scholarly effort to explain the "rise" of the West, the Industrial Revolution, the scientific revolution of the seventeenth century, or any other significant historical transformation that is believed to have contributed to this result. It is, in fact, the effort to discover just what made this enormous expansion of western productive capacities possible that has made the study of western history so significant to a generation that is trying to transform the economic bases of the undeveloped world. More scholars of every background and outlook are turning to the study of western history to reveal the secret that galvanized the West. All of them hope that careful examination of the "rise of the West" during the past several centuries will serve the interests of the rest of the world's peoples who are struggling to improve the quality of their lives. In the end, one hard truth governs all human activity: if a society does not have the capacity to produce, its people cannot hope to enjoy an improved level of well-being, whatever its ideological faith may be.

With this relevance of western history in mind, let us now examine briefly certain broad general characteristics of Western civilization that most scholars believe gave it the unique qualities that made it important in global history. Before we examine these characteristic themes of Western civilization, however, we should first try to define it within the larger framework of its historic setting.

As we have already noted, Western civilization in its most recent form is usually thought of as centering in Europe and the overseas societies that have developed out of the European tradition; however, its roots reach much farther back into the past. Western civilization is, in fact, the heir to a combination of historical traditions mainly but not entirely originating in the Mediterranean region. Although, on occasion, it has borrowed a good deal from more remote regions of Asia (particularly India and China) and Africa, its main impress has been given by the peoples of the Eurasian and African land masses who dwelt along the shores of the great inland sea during historical time. In its broadest sense Western civilization may be defined as the body of political, social, religious, and intellectual traditions developed by the people who have lived in the Mediterranean basin during the period since men first began to have a consciousness of their own historic past and future about 5,000 years ago. This cultural region originally included the Near East, North Africa, and the continent of Europe, but it later expanded to include Europe's cultural offshoots in the Western Hemisphere, Australia, New Zealand, and South Africa. Furthermore, Western civilization is the inheritor of the ancient Mediterranean civilizations—Egyptian, Mesopotamian, Hebrew, Greek, and Roman. It has been most influenced in its religious development by Judaism and Christianity, though, at certain periods and somewhat less directly, it has also felt the influence of Islam (Muhammadanism).

The broadly fundamental and unique characteristics of Western civilization, which will be treated as main themes of historic development in this book, are *five* in number:

1. Human manipulation of the world of nature (the material environment).
2. Belief in an ordered, purposeful universe and historical progress.
3. The expansion of Europe.
4. The problem of power: the emergence of the mass-oriented state as the political form of Western civilization.
5. The development of a global sense of history; emergence of the Great Revolutionary Idea.

Let us turn now to defining these themes.

A. HUMAN MANIPULATION OF THE WORLD OF NATURE (THE MATERIAL ENVIRONMENT)

The first theme runs implicitly through the whole history of mankind in every place and time. In the case of Western civilization, however, man has attained such high levels of production through his manipulation of the natural world that he sometimes has the illusion that he has truly achieved a control over nature. Although the twentieth century with its massive ecological problems has revealed how far man is from this goal, western science and technology have utilized the material resources of the natural environment in ways unparalleled by other societies or in other periods of time. The earliest moves in this direction began when man made the first crude tools and weapons and later found out how to raise food plants and to domesticate animals. Thereafter, for gaining his food or for protecting himself, he was not dependent upon the chance opportunities offered by nature. He had taken the first slow steps in the direction of winning some small control over the environment in which he lived. Since the Neolithic Revolution (which is still regarded by many historians as the most significant phase in the history of man's civilized development, see p. 19), when humans first discovered how to domesticate animals and crops, man— particularly western man—has increased his skills and knowledge, not always in a steady, progressive way but often by fits and starts, until with the coming of the modern industrial revolutions he has seemed to manipulate nature so successfully as to make it possible for him to contemplate the extension of his habitat even beyond the confines of earth itself.

Along with his technological development man has created certain institutions and social customs that have also increased his capacity to manipulate the material world. Though his sense of cooperation has not enabled him to avoid wars, man has, nonetheless, found ways of working with his fellows that give him an increasing measure of protection against natural disasters, against other forms of life, and even against other men. As a consequence, his species has flourished.

B. BELIEF IN AN ORDERED, PURPOSEFUL UNIVERSE AND HISTORICAL PROGRESS

For many historians one of the important reasons why western man has been fairly successful in his attempts to manipulate nature is that he has developed certain ways of thinking about the world in which he lives. At various stages of his history he has assumed that the universe is an orderly place where all is done according to a divine or natural law that exists over and above the welter of human affairs and behind which there is a purpose that generally works for the best despite all the contradictions and evils that seem to exist in the daily world. While this assumption of an ordered universe may not be entirely unique to western thought, nevertheless it is one outstanding characteristic and seems to derive from two main sources: first, from the Judaic tradition, later carried over into Christianity, that all of history is subject to the divine law of God; and, second, from the Greek intellectual tradition, which thought of the world, in spite of the diversity and disorder of everyday life, as a place governed by harmonious, mathematical laws. These two ideas, though they have often seemed contradictory, on the contrary were actually complementary; for they combined to form an intellectual tradition that is usually defined as "rational." What "rational" means is that not only is the universe governed by laws but that man is possessed of a "reasoning faculty" or "reason," which makes it possible for him to understand these laws and their workings. In this sense, the world is not an unknown or unknowable place controlled by sheer chance or by capricious spirits but one in which man, by placing himself voluntarily in harmony with divine or natural laws, can hope to exercise some control over his own destiny.

In the presence of this belief in an ordered and purposeful universe western man has customarily thought about "history"—that is to say, his own past and future—in a distinctive way. Since the days of the Hebrews and the Greeks he has developed what is sometimes called "historical consciousness," a sense of past and future, of knowing that things are not always alike and the same. The idea of change in human history is an important one, for many societies have never developed such a conception but think of history only as a passage of time in which all things—beliefs, customs, ideas—remain essentially the same from one age to another. For western man, however, the idea of historical change has usually implied movement toward some great divine event or a better world in the future: in Christian terms, the last judgment and the everlasting life; in secular thought, the worldly utopia where all men would live out their lives in moral perfection and material abundance. This faith in historical purpose and change, whether cast in religious or secular terms, has had important social consequences, for it has helped to spur western man onward to what he has generally, though not always, believed will be a better future. At the same time it has reconciled him to the fact of and the necessity for continuous change in his existence. While he has not always accepted such change quickly or happily, he nonetheless has accustomed himself to it and has come to believe in it to such an extent that it has often stimulated him to alter his material circumstances and to feel that in most instances change is good. Out of this feeling has grown that faith in human progress that has dominated and still strongly influences much of modern western thought.

C. THE EXPANSION OF EUROPE

A third significant theme of western history has to do with the growth or expansion of Europe. Usually, this term is applied to the movement that began about the year 1500, when the first great voyages of discovery opened up distant non-European areas to European conquest, settlement, and trade. Actually, however, the age of discovery, for all its importance, was only one phase in a much more general kind of expansion that has had both internal and external aspects. For the expansion of Europe has involved not simply the movement of European people and wealth to remote parts of the earth but also an internal expansion, which began well before the great age of discovery in the sixteenth and seventeenth centuries and has continued to our own day. This expansion, whose beginnings have been traced back as far as the opening of the eleventh century, is characterized by five major developments: (1) growth of population; (2) rise of towns and cities (increasing urbanization); (3) colonization, first of unsettled areas within Europe and later of extensive areas overseas; (4) a revolution in agricultural techniques, which gradually increased the production of food; and (5) the growth of capital wealth (that is, an accumulation of goods or money used to expand economic or business activity and thus further increase production). The last of these developments is of great significance, because the European concept of capital investment (capitalism), while it has had some good and bad effects, is one of the important economic inventions of all time and has led to a process by which economic production has continuously increased and new wealth has been steadily added to society. In varying degrees all of the five above aspects of Europe's expansion have contributed to a general process of growth throughout Western civilization not only in population but also in standards of living, in knowledge, and in political power.

What was ultimately most significant about Europe's internal expansion, however, was that it prepared the way for the discovery and colonization of vast regions beyond the seas. Without the long gestation of internal expansion from the early Middle Ages onward there would have been no possibility of Europe's breaking through the cultural isolation that characterized most human societies down to the year 1500. Wealth, technology, and the political organization of the national monarchy all played an important part, and all were developments of medieval origin. While these indirectly made outward expansion possible, Europeans still had to be motivated toward the great effort of discovery and colonization. Undoubtedly, Christian missionary zeal had strong influences, particularly among the Portuguese and Spaniards. So, too, did the more mundane desire for riches. But neither of these was a peculiarly European motivation. Nor did Europeans at the moment when expansion began have either skills or wealth beyond those possessed by some other societies. The great Chinese empire for example, as well as several Islamic societies might also have made the effort. Islam, after all, was scarcely less zealous than Christianity in its desire to convert the heathen. Chinese, Indian, or Arab traders were as anxious for wealth. Why, then, did Europe make the first moves toward creating a world community and civilization? The answer seems to lie in the fact that European motives were not only intense but that European consciousness of the unknown for some mysterious reason stimulated the curiosity and moved Europeans to action as other societies were not so stimulated or moved.

The result of this complex combination of causes was extremely significant for world history. Indeed it was European expansion that first made all the isolated cultures of the world conscious not only of themselves but of the world as a whole. Ultimately, the great success of European civilization with its utilization of science and technology, in particular, was to make for the first time a true worldwide civilization.

D.   THE PROBLEM OF POWER: THE EMERGENCE OF THE MASS-ORIENTED STATE AS THE POLITICAL FORM OF WESTERN CIVILIZATION

The fourth major theme, one that many historians regard as among the most important, deals with western man's efforts to control himself and his fellows in their workaday relations with one another. The problems of political power and the relations of the individual with the state are not, of course, things with which western man alone has had to cope. These problems are as old as organized society. What is peculiar to western man in this respect, however is his attempt to solve the problem of political power by recognizing, formally or actually, the right of the adult mass of human beings to control or influence the state and its decisions. Also recognized, so implicitly that it remains unstated in most discussions, is the function of the state to serve the desires or at least the welfare of its people. And while it is true that not all the states of the Western world are what we somewhat inaccurately call "democracies," any western government now in existence would pretend that in the ultimate its great concern is with the total well-being of all its people. Even the most totalitarian regimes justify their existence on those grounds.

One of our concerns, then, is to understand how this assumption of mass control or mass welfare came to dominate the political thinking and to a large extent the political practice of the West. In part, it may be explained by the evolution of monarchical government in early modern history (sixteenth through the eighteenth centuries), when kings ceased to be the limited, personal rulers of feudal monarchies and became instead the theoretically all-powerful heads of a state apparatus that regulated and controlled the lives of their subjects. In the course of this change, however, European monarchs found themselves facing strong opposition from an ever growing body of subjects. At first the royal claims to power were resisted by the old feudal nobility, who resented the assumption of complete political authority by the crown. Later, as wealth increased and the level of literacy rose, other classes and groups in various countries of Europe also joined in the resistance to royal authority. These persons, who generally belonged to the professional and business classes more frequently described as the "middle class" (though the term is somewhat vague), actually prepared the way for the great democratic mass movements of the nineteenth and twentieth centuries. This they could not have done, however, had not a further increase in wealth and production, attendant upon the industrialization of Europe from the eighteenth century onward, made it possible to raise the literacy level of the masses and to increase the political consciousness of large numbers of ordinary human beings. The end result is that Western civilization has been able to develop a social and political awareness that has worked in favor of the "common man" to an extent unknown in any previous historic period.

E. THE DEVELOPMENT OF A GLOBAL SENSE OF HISTORY: EMERGENCE OF THE GREAT REVOLUTIONARY IDEA

The expansion of Europe and the increasing mass orientation of most western societies has had an important impact on all the world's peoples, which could not have been foreseen when the great age of European discovery began five centuries ago. In the course of the eighteenth and nineteenth centuries the rise of mass democracy and socialism further helped to create the sense of human oneness by stressing the humanistic worth of every man, no matter how humble his place in the social order. Indeed, both democracy and democratic socialism have at the bases of their beliefs a faith in the rationality and decency of the ordinary human being, without which there could be no justification for the mass-controlled or mass-oriented state at all. From this proposition it was easy to extend the argument that all men were essentially the same except for the accident of geographic environment or social origin and that ethnic variations or differences in skin pigment were of no significant consequence in determining the essential worth of people. The French Revolution gave a strong impetus to this sense of universal humanism by the declaration in 1789 that "man" was entitled to certain inalienable rights as a human being and not as a Frenchman or Englishman or even as a European. Later it would be argued that the Declaration of the Rights of Man and the Citizen (1789) was nothing more than a statement of the rights of the French middle class (bourgeoisie) and that as such it was a narrowly restricted document that had nothing to do with the interests of the vast mass of humanity in or out of France. Nevertheless, this was not the intention of the men who wrought the French Revolution, as the language of the famous declaration clearly indicates. They were undertaking to preserve the universal sense of humanity that had been a characteristic of the Christian conception of mankind. The Church promised salvation to all without regard for differences of race, language, or social condition. The men of 1789 simply secularized that point of view and thus developed a universalized vision of mankind divorced for the first time from the limitations of religious sectarianism.

In the two generations after 1789 the spread of this idea slowly influenced the policies of even the greatest imperial states and gradually reached out to touch the consciousness of the Third World. In this fashion the European world vision slowly but surely prepared the way for the great anticolonial revolution of the twentieth century.

Another equally important element in this preparatory process was the formulation during the half century after 1789 of a new and powerful idea unique in world history, which we may call the Great Revolutionary Idea. For this idea as for the universal secularized vision of history the French Revolution was in large measure responsible, though here also the conception reached very far back into western religious thought. The Great Revolutionary Idea derived from the belief that a mighty apocalyptic upheaval of the masses could transform society permanently in such a way as to guarantee freedom, human rights, and later—in socialist and Marxian thinking—a decent level of subsistence for everyone in a social order where reorganization assured the equitable redistribution of economic production. This idea was more than just a pious hope or vague aspiration. It was rooted in an intense faith that the productive capacity of an industrializing Europe was more than sufficient to meet all human needs if it were utilized fully and its products were distributed according to need and not according to wealth or station. This conception of an abundance that was not shared widely enough among the toiling masses came to be accepted on a worldwide basis after 1914 as the anticolonialist, anti-European, revolutionary consciousness of the Third World began to develop. Just as it had been argued by the European proponents of revolutionary socialism that the workers who—as most socialists but particularly Marxian socialists saw it—were the true creators of all wealth had been exploited by the capitalist entrepreneurs of industrial Europe, so it came to be argued that European imperialism had robbed and exploited the Third World masses for the benefit of European ruling elites. Whether anti-European revolts took the form of Marxian or nationalist uprising against European rule, all of them tended to make use of some variant form of the Great Revolutionary Idea as justification for their courses of action. Thus it was that by a kind of paradox Europe and the West supplied the intellectual justification for movements that ultimately helped to destroy European hegemony over much of the earth.

chapter two

EVENTS AND DEFINITIONS

A. INTRODUCTION: THE UNIQUENESS OF MAN

In order that so complex an organism as man could come into existence a vast number of conditions had to occur during the very long period of biological evolution. Indeed, the number of biological causes that resulted in the eventual evolution of modern man is so great that we could not hope to enumerate all of them in a book many times this size. Nevertheless, certain conditions were fundamental to the geological and biological history of the earth, and without them man could never have come into being. The most important of these fundamental conditions are listed below.

1. Planetary preconditions for the existence of life.
    a. For organic life to exist, a planet must receive from its sun a constant amount of radiation.
    b. The planetary orbit must be close to circular. Orbit cannot vary appreciably; otherwise surface temperatures will fluctuate too extremely to support life.
    c. The planetary mass must not be so large as to prevent formation of a gaseous atmosphere nor so small that the atmospheric gases will

Man and His Past

THE ESSENTIAL MOVEMENT

A. INTRODUCTION: THE UNIQUENESS OF MAN

Human civilization fills a relatively short span in the biological history of mankind and an infinitesimally short one in the geological history of the planet. Man is a late-comer to the world scene. His achievements during the few hundred millennia of his existence are remarkable when one considers the fairly long periods during which other organisms dominated the earth. Man has, quite literally, exploded into biological prominence. He has detailed knowledge of only one small part of his history, roughly 5,000 recent years; he can only infer or deduce from anthropological or archeological evidence just what stages his prehistoric ancestors passed through before they became conscious that they had a future and a past. Astonishingly, despite the seemingly vast accretion of modern knowledge, men really know little about themselves, their origins, and their early evolution. The human race lives in a flash of consciousness isolated from the darkness of the past and the uncertainty of the future. For men, the greatest riddle is still that of human existence. How was it that man came to be in all the vastness of a seemingly impersonal universe? What is the purpose, if any, in his being where he is? Men have sought for bits and pieces of clues

escape easily when formed. Too small a planetary mass will also prevent the formation of water in liquid form.

   d. The planet must be stable for hundreds of millions of years so that life-forming and evolutionary processes have long periods of time in which to operate.

2. Geological evolution.

   a. Original formation of matter into earth's planetary form, about 5 billion to 10 billion years ago.

   b. Development of a biochemical environment (chemical evolution) including a certain amount of "free" oxygen available for use in biochemical processes of first primitive cellular organisms, perhaps 3.5 billion years ago.

3. Biological evolution.

Evolution of primitive cellular life from simple forms without nucleus to forms with a simple nucleus capable of independent bio-chemical existence (autotrophs). It is believed that the earliest organic forms of cell life passed through three stages which eventually made the great variety of biological life forms possible and almost explosively speeded up the processes of organic evolution. These stages were:

   a. Emergence of cellular life without nucleus (prokaryotic organisms —bacteria and blue-green algae); change from abiotic (nonorganic) to organic period when life truly began. Sometime before 3.2 billion years ago.

   b. Growth of cellular diversity among independent organisms; differences of shape and structure prepared the way for later evolutionary development. About 2 billion years ago.

   c. Emergence of cellular life with nucleus (eukaryotic organisms), which made possible sexual reproduction and an enormous expansion of the variety of organic life. Process of evolution greatly accelerated. Perhaps one billion years ago.

B. THE ORIGINS OF MAN

1. Human development to the beginning of the Paleolithic period (Old Stone Age), from about 25 million to one million years ago.

   a. Emergence of man's ancestors about 25 million years ago in the subtropics of the Old World (Africa and Asia).

   b. First hominid (manlike) creature so far discovered (*Ramapithecus*

from the beginning of recorded time,' and though the evidence has mounted, we are still far from any final answer. Each generation turns anew to the excitement and mystery of it; and each, in looking backward across human history, seeks to add some previously unknown piece of evidence or some new hypothesis that may bring men sure knowledge about their own beginnings. Whether this goal will ever be reached we cannot now know. For those who think the answers to the "big questions" about man are worth knowing, the excitement of the search is enough to justify it.

Although we seldom realize it, men are rare and wonderful creatures, if not unique in the universe (mathematical probability suggests that there may be advanced life elsewhere in the vast reaches of time and space), certainly so scarce as to be marvelled at. We are unique in the sense that we possess special capacities that, so far as we can observe, no other organism on our planet possesses. We are conscious of ourselves, our world, our past, our future; and we are capable of changing things around us, at least to some degree, for our own benefit. Furthermore, we are also capable of thinking and speculating beyond the range of our own immediate instinctive experience. Man is an evolutionary development of enormous importance because he is a restless, aggressive creature whose various capacities cause continuous change in the planetary environment and in his relations with other men and other organisms. He continually hopes to find a final stability in which all his problems will be solved permanently to the complete satisfaction of all mankind. This stability probably will never be achieved because man creates continuous change and must live with the often unforeseen results of that change. Our greatest obligation if man is to survive as a species is to understand as much as we can about ourselves and the processes that have made us and our planet as they are today. We must think on the grand scale if we are to endure, for we are increasingly aware that in the long eons of prehistory stretching back at least 20 million years there occurred patterns of development that still control our thoughts and actions in mysterious biological ways.

B. THE ORIGINS OF MAN

One of the significant and mysterious developments of the Paleolithic period (one million years ago to 12,000 B.C.) was the rapid evolutionary transformation that saw the emergence of *Homo sapiens sapiens*, or modern man. Formerly, it was thought that man's tool-using or tool-making capacities had evolved quite late in his evolutionary history

punjabicus, first found in India) appeared about 15 million years ago, living in the savannas (grasslands) that then stretched across much of Africa into Asia.

c. Major gap in our knowledge of human evolution covers the period between 14 million and 5 million years ago; for this time span we have no fossil record of any hominid forms.

d. Emergence of identifiable hominids—*Australopithecus africanus* ("southern ape of Africa") and *Australopithecus robustus* (so called from his greater size and weight)—about 4 million to 5 million years ago; fossils discovered in South Africa in 1924.

2. Human development in the Paleolithic period, from one million years ago to about 12,000 B.C. The emergence of modern man. This is the period when evolution significantly separated man from the apes; humans developed an enormously enlarged brain together with the faculties that such a brain makes possible.

a. A direct biological descendant of *Australopithecus africanus* was *Homo erectus* (Java Man, Peking Man, Heidelberg Man), a creature whose characteristics, including brain size, approximate those of modern man. About 750,000 years ago.

b. First *Homo sapiens* (Swanscombe Man, Steinheim Man) emerged about 250,000 years ago.

c. Modern or recent man (*Homo sapiens sapiens*), represented by Cro-Magnon Man, suddenly appeared in Europe some 35,000 years ago and has been dominant ever since. Where he originally evolved is still a matter of dispute and remains one of the great unsolved puzzles of human evolution.

C. THE ADVANCE OF MAN SINCE THE PALEOLITHIC PERIOD: THE NEOLITHIC REVOLUTION

1. MESOLITHIC PERIOD (MIDDLE STONE AGE), ca. 12,000 TO ca. 8000 B.C.

Recession of the last glacier; dog domesticated; bow and arrow used.

2. NEOLITHIC PERIOD (NEW STONE AGE), ca. 8000 TO 5000 B.C.

There has long been a great deal of discussion among scholars as to where the Neolithic Revolution first occurred on earth. The reason for doubt is that primitive man wherever he first organized into communities had some of the skills that characterize the Neolithic Revolution. For the present,

and that these made him distinct from the animals. It is now known, however, that tool use and even tool making are widespread in the animal kingdom and that the most distinctive characteristic of man is his large brain size and the consequent faculties of speech, memory, and abstract thought. How man's brain came to evolve so rapidly (and why it apparently stopped evolving some 300,000 years ago) has long been the subject of biological speculation.

Biologists suggest three reasons for the rapid evolutionary increase in human brain size: (1) meat eating and big-game hunting, which required inventive skills, planning, and group cooperation; (2) the use of speech to plan, coordinate, and memorize; and (3) probable polygamous structure of early breeding groups, which permitted the individual with leadership qualities to have several wives and thus produce more offspring bearing his advanced characteristics.

The emergence of modern man is also thought to have been affected by two other developments. Evidence would seem to indicate that about 100,000 years ago cultural evolution (ability to learn and to pass on accumulated knowledge) became more important than genetic evolution in the survival of the human species. It is also thought that the retreat of the great glaciers 12,000 to 14,000 years ago increased food supplies so significantly that a "population explosion" may have occurred among postglacial mankind. Both of these occurrences, but particularly cultural evolution, contributed to making man the dominant species of the planet.

C. THE ADVANCE OF MAN SINCE THE PALEOLITHIC PERIOD: THE NEOLITHIC REVOLUTION

In the earliest periods of human history, because men lacked highly developed skills and techniques, it was necessary to devote almost all of human activity to the winning of subsistence or to the protection of self, family, or tribe. With time, men acquired more highly developed skills and expanded their political organization so that relatively less time and effort had to be devoted to subsistence or protection. As a consequence, men were able to turn their attention to other things— literature, art, learning—which were not immediately useful in winning bread or in warding off enemies. Furthermore, as human social organization became more complex, the time required for the acquisition of social skills and techniques had to be extended, and education

however, the consensus of opinion is that the great transformation of the Neolithic period probably occurred first in southwestern Asia in regions near to or encompassed by the two great rivers, Tigris and Euphrates, and the region of the Indus. Why it should have first occurred in those regions is still a matter of conjecture. Two suggestions have been made. First, that this was a region in which wild cereals, later domesticated into agricultural crops, flourished in a natural state. In brief, it is believed that men, in observing the cycle of growth of these wild cereals by trial and error hit upon the idea of gathering and planting cereal seeds. Second, it is also conjectured that the inhabitants of this region were driven to undertake domestic agriculture by necessity. Evidence seems to indicate that the region passed through a prolonged period of drought as a result of major climatic changes. This drought forced men to think of new expedients for survival. One of these expedients may have been domestic agriculture. Whatever the case, the archaeological record seems to indicate that this region developed the oldest existing village communities of a kind that would not have been possible without agricultural skills.

The four major cultural attainments of the Neolithic Revolution, which is still perhaps the most important in human history, were (1) agriculture; (2) domesticated animals; (3) pottery; and (4) polished (rather than chipped) stone tools.

The great advance of the Neolithic Revolution was that it enabled man to produce a surplus of food for his ordinary needs for the first time in history.

D. THE ADVANCE OF MAN INTO THE URBAN REVOLUTION

1. CHALCOLITHIC PERIOD (COPPER AND STONE AGES), ca. 5000 TO ca. 3500 B.C.

Era of transition when metalworking began to be fairly common.

2. BRONZE AGE BEGINS, ca. 3500 B.C.

Use of copper-tin alloys marked the beginning of metallurgy and probably also the beginning of a more complex social organization leading up to the Urban Revolution.

3. URBAN REVOLUTION ca. 3000 B.C.

The achievements of the Neolithic Revolution made possible the emergence of a more sophisticated and complex social organization. Villages came into being, and, in time, villages gradually expanded into the larger units we know as cities. The city was a diversified, interdependent social unit whose

came to be an important part of social life. In time, too, it was less necessary for every able-bodied person to participate directly in the gathering or growing of food, so that men were able to diversify their social organization in such a way that some persons became specialists in technique. This development had two important results: first, it led to the formation of a specialized social system with a class structure whose various components usually had a specific function to fulfill; and, second, it ultimately made possible the greater concentration of human population in towns and cities.

Almost all these changes occurred before the beginning of recorded history as a result of two great revolutions in human activity, the Neolithic and urban revolutions.

The first of these is usually called the Neolithic Revolution because it was the culmination of a development at the end of the Stone Age by which men became food producers rather than food gatherers. Men learned to improve their earliest stone tools by grinding and polishing; they also learned to domesticate animals and to cultivate crops, achievements that made them far less dependent upon the caprices of nature and thus gave them, in a limited way, some control over their environment. As a result of the Neolithic Revolution the number of people who could survive to raise families was enormously increased, and men eventually spread themselves over the face of the earth into virtually every area that was capable of supporting human life.

D. THE ADVANCE OF MAN INTO THE URBAN REVOLUTION

Following the Neolithic Revolution mankind appears to have passed through two stages of technological development leading up to and co-incident with the rise of city life. The first of these stages is usually described as the Bronze Age because during this period men first began to make use of metals, specifically of copper and tin, which go into the making of bronze. The second stage saw the introduction of ironworking and is therefore known as the Iron Age. Using these metals—stronger and more durable than stone—men began to develop tools and skills that, in their turn, made possible the Urban Revolution: the emergence of that more complex social form known as a civilization.

At this point we need to understand what the words "culture" and "civilization" mean. Despite a great many differences among scholars, the term "culture" is most frequently employed to describe the social life of a community in a preliterate stage—that is, before it has acquired the skills of reading and writing. "Civilization," on the

existence depended upon the development of various kinds of specialized skills. Moreover, the city was a social organism that could not support itself without access to surplus foods and raw materials not produced within the city itself. Cities therefore had to live by specialized manufacture and external trade. The growth of specialization brought into being various groups previously unknown to rural communities or even villages. Artisans, priests, officials and soldiers could not have existed in previous communities. Furthermore, the complexities of city life and the needs of government, commerce, and manufacture required literacy. Without literacy in the forms of writing, reading, and mathematics it would have been impossible to conduct trade across great distances or to govern larger territories. It is not surprising, therefore, that the emergence of city life throughout the Near and Middle East sometime around 4000 B.C. also ushered in the beginnings of written language and the development of arithmetical skills.

4.   IRON AGE BEGINS, ca. 1800 B.C.

Last major stage in the early development of metallurgy.

other hand, is commonly descriptive of communities that have reached the stage of literacy and have developed a number of the complex ideas (art and science, for example) and institutions that give society a measure of stability and efficiency in the handling of social problems.

The city is preeminently the symbol of civilization. With the coming of city life, the community ceases to be a small, isolated, homogeneous, self-sufficient unit. The division of labor is no longer simple. Relationships among people transcend personal or family ties and become impersonal and indirect. The city itself is dependent upon, but exists in partial isolation from, the surrounding countryside. Its ideas and values are often very different, and in the long run a city's influence will often transform its rural surroundings completely. Once the city has come into being, man is equipped with a social organization capable of transmitting new ideas and innovations across great distances, for the city becomes not only the great innovator of civilizations but also the means by which they are spread across the world.

chapter three

EVENTS AND DEFINITIONS

A. THE CIVILIZATIONS OF THE TIGRIS-EUPHRATES REGION (MESOPOTAMIA)

1. EARLY COPPER AGE, ca. 4500–3000 B.C.

Invention of writing; period of primitive democratic societies.

2. EARLY SUMERIAN CIVILIZATION; HEGEMONY OF AKKADIANS, ca. 3000–2000 B.C.

Formation of separate city-states by about 3000 B.C. Akkadians under Sargon and Naram-Sin ruled over most of Sumeria, ca. 2400–2250 B.C. Sumerians disappeared as a separate people, ca. 2000 B.C.

Sumerian Religion. The earliest Mesopotamian historical records reveal that the first social units were temple communities that the king and the

The Early Civilizations
of the Eastern
Mediterranean

THE ESSENTIAL MOVEMENT

The oldest civilizations known to western man are two that grew up in the great river-valley systems of the Nile and the Tigris-Euphrates. Both areas provided an environment (soil, water, climatic conditions) conducive to a high level of social development. There, so far as we know, man gained his earliest experience of civilized urban life.

A. THE CIVILIZATIONS OF THE TIGRIS-EUPHRATES REGION (MESOPOTAMIA)

Between the Tigris and Euphrates rivers in what is now the kingdom of Iraq appeared the first sophisticated urban societies of the Neolithic Revolution. There, a sweeping arc of land (the fertile crescent) watered by the two great rivers cradled the societies out of which later western civilization was to evolve. Unlike Egypt, which is discussed in the next section, the Tigris-Euphrates region was not defined by the clear geophysical limits of a single river valley. The rivers flowed for long distances through open plains and were neither so easily managed for human use nor so predictable in their flood stages as the Nile. This somewhat harsher environment influenced the formation of a system

priests ruled as agents of the gods. Thus there was no such thing in ancient Mesopotamia as a secular state in the modern sense. The life of the people was controlled and permeated by religion as fully as was the life of Egypt, but with an important difference. While the gods of Egypt tended, on the whole, to be beneficent, the gods of Sumer were not only capricious but, in a sense, indifferent to man's fate. According to the Sumerian legend of creation, mankind was created to serve the gods. Man was thus a slave to divine authority, and even kings were only stewards responsive to the will of the gods. The gods were worshipped out of fear and submission and not because men loved them. The gods of Mesopotamia were not looked upon as just and powerful protectors who rewarded good and punished evil. The gods, in fact, did not protect the land nor behave justly to its inhabitants. They demanded much of their worshippers and gave little in return. Believers offered sacrifices to the gods to avoid divine wrath. The gods, furthermore, never made it clear just what they wanted from their followers. It was up to ordinary men to guess what the gods wanted of them and woe betide if they were wrong. In this respect the gods of Mesopotamia differed from the Hebrews' conception of divinity. The Hebrew God required certain things of his people but always made it perfectly clear just what it was he expected. As a result, the ancient Hebrews even in times of tribulation always had a sense of confidence and security that the Sumerians never possessed. The Sumerian sense of pessimism was perhaps best expressed in the *Epic of Gilgamesh*, wherein the hero overcomes great difficulties in a search for immortality, only to lose the precious gift in the end by sheer chance. The lesson of the great epic is plain: There is no end for man in this world but death.

3. BABYLONIAN SUPREMACY, ca. 2000–910 B.C.

a. **Rule of the Amorites, ca. 2000–1750 B.C.**   Babylon asserted supremacy over most of the Tigris-Euphrates region; Marduk became chief god of Mesopotamia; Code of Hammurabi formulated, ca. 1800 B.C.

b. **Rule of the Kassites, ca. 1750–910 B.C.**

4. ASSYRIAN EMPIRE, ca. 910–606 B.C.

Conquest of Babylon by Assyrians (910 B.C.). Conquest of Samaria and deportation of its inhabitants, ca. 721 B.C. Conquest of Egypt by Esar-Haddon, ca. 670 B.C. Assyrians defeated and their empire overthrown at Battle of Carchemish, ca. 606 B.C.

5. CHALDEANS AND NEW BABYLONIANS, 606–538 B.C.

Nebuchadnezzar conquered Jerusalem, 586 B.C. Persian conquest of Babylon, 538 B.C.

of beliefs and institutions very different from those of ancient Egypt. In general, the gods of Mesopotamia (another name for the region) were less benign and more capricious than the Egyptian deities. As a consequence, the literature of the early Mesopotamian peoples is filled with a pessimistic fear of the inexplicable wrath of the gods.

In the earliest known stages of its history the civilization of Mesopotamia was dominated by the Sumerians, who lived in a confederation of city-states, which were finally brought together under the rule of a single people, the Akkadians, about 3000 B.C. The hegemony of the Akkadians was followed by a series of foreign conquests until sometime around 2300 B.C., when the city of Ur was able to achieve independence and bring the other Sumerian cities under its control. Around 2000 B.C. a new group of conquerors, the Amorites, captured Babylon on the Euphrates and gradually made this small village into the center of the Sumerian world. During the period immediately following the Amorite conquest the city-god of Babylon, Marduk, supplanted the other deities of Sumer, and Hammurabi, the sixth king of the new dynasty, gave a famous code of laws to the whole Tigris-Euphrates region. After Hammurabi's death (about 1750 B.C.) a new band of barbarians, the Kassites, conquered Babylon and ruled it and the surrounding territories until the kingdom of Assyria emerged as the dominant power of the Middle East in the tenth century B.C.

With the coming of the Assyrians the whole of the eastern Mediterranean area was for the first time united into a single great empire. The Assyrians, because of their ruthless passion for conquest and the harshness with which they treated defeated peoples, were the most hated conquerors of the ancient world. Nonetheless, their military and administrative skills have to be admired, for these enabled the Assyrians to branch out from their capital at Nineveh on the upper reaches of the Tigris to bring Mesopotamia, Palestine, and Egypt under their control during the eighth and seventh centuries B.C. In the end, their capacity as conquerors exceeded their ability to control the territories they had absorbed. Their final defeat came toward the end of the seventh century at the hands of the Chaldeans, who had settled in the southeastern corner of the Tigris-Euphrates valley.

The empire built by the Chaldeans, in spite of its great cultural achievements, was short-lived. Internal decay led to its easy overthrow in 538 B.C. by Cyrus (ca. 600–529 B.C.), the Great King of the Medes and Persians, and the foundation by these latter peoples of another great empire stretching from the Hellespont to the river Indus. This conquest led to the merging of the civilizations of the ancient Mesopotamian and Mediterranean worlds into the mainstream of Western

The Civilizations of the Tigris-Euphrates Region   27

6. PERSIAN EMPIRE, ca. 600–330 B.C.

Prophet Zoroaster preached a highly ethical and humane religion, ca. 600 B.C. Conquest of Egypt by Persians, 525 B.C. Attempts to conquer Greece by Darius the Great (521–486 B.C.) and Xerxes (486–465 B.C) defeated at Marathon (490 B.C.) and Salamis (480 B.C.). Alexander the Great conquered Persia, 330 B.C.

7. THE MESOPOTAMIAN CULTURAL ACHIEVEMENT

The importance of the Mesopotamian cultural achievement as it evolved from ancient Sumer to the Persians is difficult to exaggerate. The peoples of the region developed the first writing, the first true alphabet, commercial organization, city-state government, weights and measures, a numbering system based upon the unit 60, which later resulted in the 360-degree circle, and a codified system of law.

B. THE EGYPTIAN CIVILIZATION

1. OLD KINGDOM: DYNASTIES I–VI, ca. 3000–2200 B.C.

Union of Upper and Lower Egypt, ca. 3200 B.C. First great era of pyramid building (Great Pyramid of Cheops or Khufu, ca. 2600 B.C.). Evolution of the divine kingship of Pharaoh.

2. FIRST INTERMEDIATE PERIOD: DYNASTIES VII–XI, ca. 2200–2000 B.C.

civilization, for it was Darius the Great (521–486 B.C.) who, having usurped the Persian throne on the death of Cyrus's successor, conquered Egypt and attempted the conquest of a part of Europe in a series of unsuccessful campaigns against the Greek city-states.

While it is impossible to say just how much the various societies of the Tigris-Euphrates region and the later empires into which they were absorbed influenced Hellenic (Greek) civilization and thus, ultimately, the civilization of the Western world, there seems little doubt but that there must have been a great deal of interchange that had lasting effects. The Mesopotamian civilization was a seed-bed of numerous important religions, including Zoroastrianism and Mithraism, both of which had certain elements in common with Judaism and Christianity and both of which later penetrated deeply into the Roman world. In other areas of culture, particularly astronomy and mathematics (in which areas the Mesopotamian civilizations appear to have excelled even the Egyptians), the influence was at least as great. Finally, it should be remembered that both the Assyrian and Persian empires developed the art of government to a level not again to be achieved in the Mediterranean world until the emergence of imperial Rome.

Probably the most important single contribution of the Mesopotamian civilization to the West and to world civilization was the evolution of writing and record keeping, although the honors in this respect must probably be shared with the Egyptians. Writing did not have an immediate universal effect, and for many centuries the largest amount of mass communication was still conducted orally. But the ability to preserve records and accounts across the generations enormously strengthened man's sense of his own awareness. The development of literacy gave mankind the corporate memory that we call "history." It is not surprising, therefore, that for centuries men should have thought that creation itself occurred about the time (ca. 4000 B.C.) when record keeping came into existence.

B. THE EGYPTIAN CIVILIZATION

Far to the west of the Tigris-Euphrates region in the long narrow valley of the Nile, which extended for hundreds of miles inland from the Mediterranean shoreline at the extreme northeastern corner of Africa, appeared another of the first true civilizations. Protected by the surrounding desert and served by the river, the ancient inhabitants of Egypt at a very early period developed a high level of agriculture, which in turn made it possible for the valley to support a fairly dense

Breakdown of central government caused disunity and localized rule.

3.   MIDDLE KINGDOM: DYNASTY XII, ca. 2000–1790 B.C.

High point of Egyptian civilization; strong central government; relatively high standard of living.

4.   SECOND INTERMEDIATE PERIOD: DYNASTIES XIII–XVII, ca. 1790–1550 B.C.

Egypt conquered by the Hyksos (shepherd kings); reconquered by Theban princes.

5.   NEW KINGDOM: PERIOD OF IMPERIAL EXPANSION, DYNASTIES XVIII–XX, ca. 1550–1090 B.C.

Conquest of Syria and part of Mesopotamia by Thutmose III (ca. 1490–1436 B.C.) at the battle of Megiddo (ca. 1468 B.C.).

a.   Book of the Dead, ca. 1400 B.C.   The *Book of the Dead* contained spells and magic formulas for entering into life after death.

b.   The Religious Revolution of Akhnaton (Ikhnaton), fourteenth century B.C.   Amenhotep IV (ca. 1377–1360 B.C.) took the name Akhnaton and tried to substitute the new, more ethically developed religion of Aton for that of Amon. Bitter resistance by the priesthood of Amon led to the restoration of the older religion after Akhnaton's death.

The cult of Aton has often been looked upon as truly monotheistic and ethical in the same sense as the religion of the ancient Hebrews. In the two great hymns to Aton which have survived there are indeed some evidences of monotheism. Aton is frequently represented as the only real god who gives and conserves life. He is also a universal and beneficent god who has been fully revealed in the heart of Akhnaton himself. Nevertheless, Aton was not like the divinities of the great monotheistic religions. He remained a nature god, as is revealed by the hymns themselves. While the hymns emphasize the importance of truth, they have no great ethical content. In this respect, they differ very markedly from the great Hebrew psalms and prophecies. Indeed, though the history of Egyptian religion indicates that there was a great deal of ethical growth over a long period of time, ethical standards remained distinctly selfish. They stressed material rewards here or in the hereafter and magnified the importance of human approval for one's personal conduct. There was little notion that duty and righteousness were good things in and of themselves. Magic was supremely important in the affairs of men both in this world and the next. The whole elaborate Osirian ritual of the dead seems, in fact, to have been designed as a means of deceiving the divine judge. For all of this, however, it must be admitted

population and to build up a complex but highly stable society that lasted for nearly 2,500 years.

The political history of ancient Egypt begins with the union of the Upper and Lower kingdoms under a single ruler about 3200 B.C. From that time onward Egyptian history is marked into periods according to the dynasties that ruled the country. The first six of these constituted the period of the Old Kingdom (ca. 3000–2200 B.C.), when a high level of civilization was first attained. Over some centuries, during the period of the Old Kingdom, the Egyptian concept of divine government evolved, and the king or pharaoh came to be looked upon as the personification of divinity. Accordingly, every form of political and social activity was pervaded with religious feeling.

After the downfall of the Old Kingdom and a period of anarchy from the VIIth through the XIth dynasties (ca. 2200–2000 B.C.), the shattered power of the pharaohs was restored; and a new period, that of the Middle Kingdom (ca. 2000–1790 B.C.), began. The Middle Kingdom marks the high point of Egyptian civilization when the mass of the people seem to have enjoyed good government and a relatively high level of prosperity. Its end came with conquest by the nomadic Hyksos who ruled the country during the Second Intermediate Period (ca. 1790–1550 B.C.). When, in time, the Egyptians learned to use the military techniques of their conquerors, native rule was gradually restored and the last great period of Egyptian history began, that of the New Kingdom (ca. 1550–1090 B.C.).

Under the dynasts of the New Kingdom much of the former strength of the pharaohs was recovered and Egypt, through the conquests of her rulers, became a great imperial power. With this external transformation, Egyptian society underwent several changes. For the first time the cultural isolation of the country was broken as Egyptians came into contact with alien societies. Increased military obligations and a great influx of foreign slaves created a new society where there was greater cleavage between rich and poor. And, finally, the priesthood of Amon (supreme god among the deities of Egypt) grew so rich and powerful that it tempted the Pharaoh Amenhotep IV, also known as Akhnaton or Ikhnaton, to break its power (ca. 1375). To do so, he tried to bring about a religious revolution by emphasizing monotheism (worship of one god) instead of the traditional polytheism (worship of many gods) of his people. Ultimately he was defeated, but the victory of the priesthood was costly. In the end, it led to the degeneration of religious belief and a consequent decline in the whole of Egyptian civilization.

By about 1150 B.C. the great Egyptian empire had begun to break

that the Egyptians had some sense of the moral order of things centuries before other peoples of the ancient world did.

c. Egyptian Cultural Achievement. The Egyptians were not great theoreticians in the field of science. Rather they were very shrewd observers who derived a great deal of their learning from practical experience. Their system of mathematics, though cumbersome, was nonetheless accurate, and they were able to use it very skillfully in engineering calculations. The greatest of their construction achievements, the Great Pyramid of Cheops (Khufu), in its measurements indicates that they possessed mathematical knowledge that would not be known in the Western world until centuries later. Their literature generally was not good narrative, because its purpose was not to tell a story but to teach timeless truths. Perhaps their greatest achievements were in the realm of architecture; they were the first ancient people to employ stone in massive construction.

6. NEW KINGDOM POST-IMPERIAL PERIOD:
DYNASTIES XXI–XXX, ca. 1090–525 B.C.

Conquest of Egypt by the Assyrians (ca. 670 B.C.); by Persia (525 B.C.); and by Alexander the Great (332 B.C.).

C. THE EASTERN MARITIME CIVILIZATIONS AND THE ANCIENT HEBREWS

1. AEGEAN (CRETAN OR MINOAN) CIVILIZATION, ca. 3000–1200 B.C.

Minoan civilization flourished on Crete, ca. 3000–1200 B.C. Mycenean (named for its capital at Mycenae) civilization appeared on Greek mainland before 1600 B.C. Conquest of Crete by Dorian invaders, ca. 1200 B.C. Dark age of Aegean civilization in Crete and on Greek mainland, ca. 1100–800 B.C.

2. HITTITES, 3000–1200 B.C.

Settled in northern Asia Minor; Hittite Empire reached its height about 1900 B.C.; overthrown about 1200 B.C.

up. During the next four centuries Egypt was, once again, ruled by a succession of foreign conquerors. Independence was restored for a brief period during the seventh and sixth centuries B.C., only to be lost to the conquering Persians in 525 B.C.

Like most ancient civilizations, that of Egypt was deeply rooted in religious belief. Under what seem to have been environmental influence, the Egyptians developed a body of rites, which symbolized on the one hand the rise and fall of the river (cult of Osiris) and on the other the power of the life-giving sun (cult of Ra). The worship of Ra became the basis for the divine authority of the pharaohs, while that of Osiris gave rise to the cult of the dead with its elaborate tomb building and mummification. Over the centuries a fairly steady progression from polytheism to monotheism is noticeable in Egyptian religious history; and with it a greater stress on ethical teaching also developed.

It is difficult to say whether Egyptian civilization had an important direct influence on the Western world. Its literature was extensive, and its achievements in mathematics (particularly in surveying and measurement), engineering (the great tombs and pyramids), and medicine are impressive even by modern standards. How much of this was transmitted directly to Western civilization we can only guess, since most of the learning of ancient Egypt had first to pass through the hands of the Greeks and Romans, who did not always acknowledge the Egyptian sources. Nonetheless, Egypt's great accomplishments over more than 2,000 years cannot have failed to make an impact on her neighbors.

C. THE EASTERN MARITIME CIVILIZATIONS AND THE ANCIENT HEBREWS

Along the shores and in the islands of the eastern Mediterranean there grew up, from about 2000 B.C. onward, a spectrum of cultures, partly maritime and partly pastoral. The two most famous maritime cultures were those of the Minoans, builders of a great oceanic empire (thalassocracy) based upon the island of Crete, whose civilization lasted from about 3000 B.C. to 1200 B.C.; and the Phoenicians, famous traders who occupied a narrow coastal strip of Palestine and Syria, which contained the great cities of Tyre and Sidon. To the north of the Phoenicians were the lands held by the Hittites (ca. 3000–1200 B.C.) and the kingdom of Lydia, which was absorbed into the Persian empire about 547 B.C. Because of their close connection with the ancient Hebrews, a

3. PHOENICIANS, SOMETIME BEFORE 2000 TO 332 B.C.

Settled in Palestine sometime before 2000 B.C. Reached the high point of maritime supremacy, ca. 1000–774 B.C. Their city, Tyre, conquered by Alexander the Great, 332 B.C.

4. ARAMAEANS, ca. 1500–732 B.C.

First appeared in Palestine about 1500 B.C. Established kingdom of Damascus (ca. 1000–732 B.C.). Damascus conquered by Assyrians, 732 B.C.

5. LYDIAN EMPIRE, ca. 950–547 B.C.

Emerged about 1000 B.C. in northern Asia Minor. Absorbed into Persian Empire, ca. 547 B.C.

6. HEBREWS, ca. 2000 B.C.–A.D. 135

Exodus of Hebrews from Egypt, ca. 1260 B.C. Period of Judges in Israel, ca. 1225–1020 B.C. Saul, king of Israel, 1020–1004 B.C. David, 1004–965 B.C. Solomon, 965–926 B.C. Division of Israel, 926 B.C. Exile of the Hebrews in Babylon, 586–538 B.C. Conquest of Palestine by Alexander the Great, 332 B.C., and by Antiochus III of Syria, 198 B.C. Revolt of the Maccabees against Antiochus IV, 167 B.C.

Roman conquest of Palestine, 63 B.C. Jewish revolt against Romans, A.D. 66–70. Destruction of Jerusalem by Emperor Titus, A.D. 70. Jews not permitted to live in rebuilt city of Jerusalem; beginning of dispersion (diaspora) of the Jewish people, A.D. 135.

The Evolution of the Hebraic Religious Tradition. One of the interesting problems of ancient history is the question of why it was that the ancient Hebrews (who later established the kingdoms of Israel and Judah) came to think of their God as a single deity whose authority extended not just over the Israelites but over all of mankind. Traditionally, of course, the answer to this puzzle, so far as believing Jews and Christians have been concerned, is simple and straightforward. The ancient Hebrews and Israelites did not "invent" the conception of monotheism. Yahweh (Jehovah) was and is the one true God of all the universe. When he revealed his purposes and his law to Abraham, he did so because the Hebrews were his people, specially chosen to impart a knowledge of divine law and of Yahweh himself to all men. The reason why Yahweh chose them for this great purpose was because they had agreed to keep his laws for all time coming. Secular historians, in the main, do not disagree with the idea that the ancient Hebrews and Israelites were unique in their monotheistic beliefs and their system of ethics. They have, however, sought to explain the "monotheistic revolution" in ancient Hebrew thought in historical rather

more important people in this general area were the Aramaeans, who were apparently one of the several Semitic tribes that first moved into Palestine about 1500 B.C. Like the Phoenicians they founded a mercantile community, whose major city was Damascus. The social resiliency and commercial importance of the Aramaeans kept them from absorption by various conquerors and over some centuries enabled them to spread their influence so widely throughout the Near East that in time their language became the common tongue of many diverse peoples and was spoken even by Jesus Christ.

So far as the future of mankind was concerned, however, the most important of the maritime peoples were the Phoenicians, because they were responsible for one of the greatest human cultural inventions—the alphabet. There is evidence for believing that other peoples may have hit upon a similar device at about the same time, but the Phoenician system ultimately triumphed and, with variations and adjustments, was more widely adopted than any other alphabetic system. What is the significance of an alphabetic system of writing as opposed to systems that use picture signs or symbols to express each word or idea in a written language? The answer must suggest itself immediately to a thoughtful reader. A pictographic or ideographic system of writing must have a separate and distinct symbol for every word or idea in a particular language vocabulary. Thus any highly developed language system of this kind—Chinese, for example—will contain many thousands of word symbols, all of which have to be explicitly memorized because the word symbol bears no relation to the way in which a word is pronounced. The advantage of an alphabet is that each letter represents a particular vocal sound, which, when written out, may be pronounced, by simply looking at the word (in theory, at least—there are many exceptions in any modern language). In an alphabetic system only a few basic letters or sound symbols are needed (twenty-four or twenty-six in most standard alphabetic systems), for they may be combined almost endlessly to form new words. The simplicity and flexibility of the alphabetic device over the centuries made possible the extension of mass literacy by making it unnecessary to learn thousands of pictographic characters in order to read and write. In short, the alphabet prepared the way for mass written communication as nothing else could have done. It is not surprising, therefore, that the Greeks, who borrowed the alphabet from the Phoenicians, looked upon the alphabet as a special gift from the gods, as later did the Romans.

Among all the peoples of the Near Eastern world, however, none was destined to a greater historical future than the Hebrew inhabitants of the Biblical land of Canaan, despite the fact that they were neither

than purely religious terms. Some scholars have suggested that the Hebrews must have been influenced by other peoples and religions in the ancient world—e.g., the Egyptian cult of Aton or Zoroastrianism. However this may be, the fact remains that the Hebrew monotheism as it developed over a period of about 600 years (from the eighth to the second century B.C.) was a product of the ancient Israelite tradition alone.

The Judaic religious tradition derived its enormous influence in large part from the truly amazing ability of the Jewish community to preserve its identity, despite the deportation of the inhabitants of the kingdom of Judah to Mesopotamia (586 B.C.) and the final dispersion (diaspora) enforced by imperial Rome in the second century A.D. The Jew carried his sense of identity through history in the form of his religious faith with its ethical code set forth in the Talmud and its family-oriented ritual practices. Since the Jews could never hope to be more than a tiny majority in the world of the diaspora, they needed a total conviction that theirs is a "true" faith and that no matter how tragic things might seem at any given moment, life must always turn out for the best because it is all a part of Yahweh's divine plan. Their conception of themselves as a "chosen people" contributed mightily to the preservation of their hopes, because it convinced the believing Jew that whatever might happen to him, the future of his people was safe in the hands of a divine power whose special concern was the upholding of the Jewish people through every vicissitude. The intensity of this conviction can alone account for a phenomenon that has puzzled historians; i.e., how a people without a geographic homeland could maintain both a religious belief and an ethnic identity for centuries after they were separated from the land in which that religion and identity had first come into existence. The fact that the Jews were able to do this had a number of significant consequences. Not only did the Jewish identity question become a serious one in the larger non-Jewish communities where Jews lived over the centuries but the very intensity of Jewish faith required that in the most adverse of circumstances Jews think hopefully about history and man's future. Messianic hope (the hope of ultimate deliverance by a divinely inspired "king of the Jews" who would establish a righteous social order, a new heaven and a new earth) was thus a creation of Jewish thought, which, when carried over into Christianity, helped give to the western historical outlook its peculiarly optimistic futuristic outlook (see p. 71). Israel's God was the God of history whose divine plan for the human race could never be evil. As articulated through the centuries by faithful Jews and Christians, this great central idea became the basis of a conception of universal history as well as of the idea of historical perfectability or progress (see pp. 7–8).

so powerful nor so cultivated as the great states that surrounded them; for the Hebrews, like the Greeks and Romans who followed after them, were to contribute significantly to Western civilization. Much of what we know about the early history of this people is derived by conjecture, based upon their cumulative historical-religious records known to the Western world as the Old Testament. From what later generations have been able to reconstruct on the basis of Biblical scholarship and archaeology, it seems plain that the Hebrews, after some centuries of warfare during which a part of their number was carried off into Egypt, founded the community of Israel sometime in the thirteenth century B.C. After a long process of evolution the various tribes of early Hebrews organized a strong kingdom, which reached its peak during the successive reigns of Saul, David, and Solomon (ca. 1020-926 B.C.). With Solomon's death, the kingdom was divided into two separate states: Israel in the north and Judah in the south. In the eighth century B.C. the northern kingdom was absorbed by Assyria. In the south, however, Judah proved more resilient; and there the Hebrew tradition was preserved, despite successive conquests by Chaldeans, Persians, and Romans. Until their final dispersion by the Romans in A.D. 70 the Hebrews or Jews (from the name Judah) augmented and expanded the religious tradition that was to make them one of the great peoples of history.

In the sphere of religion this small hill people offered the world something unique. Their religion, which appears to have been monotheistic in form as far back as historical evidence runs, gradually evolved into a system of belief quite different from the beliefs of other ancient peoples. What gave to the Hebraic religion its significant qualities was a combination of three important elements: first, a sense of purpose in history that, unlike the religions of Egypt or Mesopotamia, made it clear that man was not the victim of capricious gods moved by human passions but a being who was part of a divine plan in which the Hebrews, specifically, and later all the human race had a part to play; second, a belief that this great plan required the ethical cooperation of mankind (that is, that men were expected to make a choice in all their actions of good rather than evil); and third, the assurance that the Hebrew god, Jehovah (Yahweh), was not only omnipotent (all-powerful) but all-perfect as well. The essence of Hebrew belief was summed up in a carefully formulated code of ritualistic laws derived from the ethical teachings of the prophet Moses (decalogue, or Ten Commandments). In the end, it was the great central idea of Judaism as expressed in this code—i.e., that man was responsible to God for his transgression of the law, that was carried over into Christianity and the western tradition.

chapter four

EVENTS AND DEFINITIONS

A. THE GREEK (HELLENIC) CIVILIZATION, ca. 1300–338 B.C.

1. EARLY INVASIONS, ca. 1300–1000 B.C.

Achaeans, Ionians, Aeolians, and Epirots, ca. 1300–1100 B.C. Dorians, ca. 1100–1000 B.C.

The Background of Classical Greek Civilization. Until about 100 years ago all that was known about the beginnings of Greek civilization came down to us from the ancient Greeks themselves. This knowledge was extremely limited. The Greeks, like most early peoples, were not good record keepers, and not all the records that did exist have survived. Furthermore, the ancient Greeks did not always distinguish fact from myth or legend.

Greco-Roman Civilization

THE ESSENTIAL MOVEMENT

Two other great civilizations complete the fusion of elements in the ancient Mediterranean basin that was the foundation of Western civilization: Greece, where a very high level of culture was reached in the fifth and fourth centuries B.C.; and Rome, which, by bringing the whole Mediterranean area under its control, transmitted the traditions of the ancient world to the Christian West.

A. THE GREEK (HELLENIC) CIVILIZATION

The civilization of ancient Hellas (Greece) was centered in a geographical area made up of what is now modern Greece, the nearby islands and coastal regions of the Aegean Sea, and also settlements in western Asia Minor and along the southern shores of the Sea of Marmora. From this original homeland Greek traders and colonists moved outward until by the middle of the sixth century B.C. the Hellenes (Greeks) were scattered in settlements that extended from the Black Sea to Spain, North Africa, Europe, and Asia Minor.

The Greeks as a separately identified people first emerged some-

Thus it was necessary for scholars to reconstruct what they knew about the origins of Greek society from a few scattered sources, such as writings of Homer and Hesiod. Nevertheless, for all their limitations, these writings had an important historic effect. Homer's great poems, the *Iliad* and the *Odyssey*, helped to bring modern archaeology into being. The nineteenth-century German scholar, Heinrich Schliemann (1822–1890), was convinced that Homer's story of the siege of Troy was based upon fact. He set out to prove his hypothesis in 1870 by excavating the mount of Hissarlik in Asia Minor, which he identified as the original site of Homeric Troy. Successive excavations tended to prove Schliemann right, but, more important, they stimulated other scholars to make use of the spade as a means of expanding our knowledge of Greek prehistory. As a result, since about 1900 we have come to know more about the ancestors of the Greeks than the ancient Greeks did themselves. What do we know? Our knowledge even now is somewhat vague because we must infer a great deal from archaeological remains (artifacts), but still it is substantial. This knowledge has recently been supplemented by the studies of linguistics experts, who have translated documents like the famous Linear B fragment. It is now believed that the ancestors of the classical Greeks probably appeared in Asia Minor and the Greek mainland sometime around 2000 B.C. This, if true, suggests that the prehistory of the Greeks reaches further back into the past than scholars previously thought. Moreover, it also suggests that the great civilizations that came into being on the island of Crete and on the Greek mainland at Mycenae were in time absorbed, perhaps by conquest, into Greek society. Indeed, in the latter part of their history they probably were Greek. Sometime about 1300–1200 B.C., however, a great wave of migrations spread over the whole eastern Mediterranean region. As a consequence, there occurred a number of wars of conquest in which older, long-established societies were overthrown. The brilliant Mycenean civilization was conquered by the Dorians, a people of Greek stock but apparently little touched by the influences of other Greek societies. With the downfall of Mycenae and the collapse of its sophisticated system of government bureaucracy, the original Greek language of the Linear B fragment appears to have been lost. Thus Greek society became fragmented and entered a "dark age" from which it did not begin to emerge until the evolution of a new language—classical Greek—ushered in the era of true Hellenic civilization about the middle of the eighth century B.C.

2. HOMERIC PERIOD, ca. 850–700 B.C.

Homer's *Iliad* and *Odyssey*, ca. 850 B.C. Hesiod's poems, ca. 700 B.C.

time about the year 1000 B.C. Where they came from remains something of a mystery, but it is believed that successive waves of Greeks invaded the lower Balkan peninsula and there settled in separate tribal regions named for each group of invaders (Achaeans, Aeolians, Dorians, Epirots, and Ionians). The last of these conquerors were the Dorians, whose coming ushered in a period of transition between the end of the brilliant Mycenean civilization (an offshoot of the Minoan civilization, which had expanded from Crete to the Greek mainland) and the great age of Hellenic civilization which began about the eighth century B.C. The two great epic poems of Homer, the *Iliad* and the *Odyssey*, were written toward the end of this transitional period— probably sometime between 850 and 700 B.C. These two great works were to influence the whole cast of Greek thought and action. Man, in the Homeric tradition, is a creature whose powers are limited by the laws of fate, which neither he nor the gods can transcend. The most that human beings can hope to do is to live so that they will be immortalized, not in an afterlife but in the memory of posterity. Their duty is to live nobly and not attempt to challenge the fates by exalting themselves. To exalt oneself is to invite the retribution of the gods who administer but do not control the laws of the universe. Within this view is contained all that is essential for Greek religious belief and all the famous elements of later Greek tragedy.

At the end of the Homeric Age the distinctive characteristics of Greek society—its great variety and its lack of political unity—were already clearly in evidence. The earliest form of political organization was probably tribal. Over a period of some centuries the tribe or clan passed over into the peculiarly Greek political unit, the city-state or polis. Each polis was self-sufficient and included both an urban core and large areas of surrounding countryside. Every freeborn Greek was born into a polis just as he was born into a family. The polis was the center of life and the focus of all community activity. In this way, the city-state came to be a social as well as a political unit, and exile from the polis became the worst of all punishments. Cut off from his native city, the Hellene became a rootless person who could rarely hope to be accepted elsewhere.

The two greatest of these city-states were Sparta and Athens, each of which, in its own way, represented an extreme of cultural tradition and social organization within Greek civilization. Other cities at times challenged their supremacy, but none was so powerful or so influential as these two. Sparta, which was early organized into a quasi-military society where the freeborn citizens (Spartiates) controlled a much

3. EARLY GREEK EXPANSION AND COLONIZATION

Asia Minor, ca. 1100–900 B.C. Sicily and southern Italy (Magna Graecia), ca. 800–600 B.C. Black Sea (Euxine) area, 756–747 B.C.

4. SPARTA

Enslavement of the Messenians made possible the founding of Sparta, ca. 736–716 B.C. Legendary "Lycurgus the Lawgiver" drew up a severe Spartan social and military code, ca. 610 B.C. Spartans victorious in Peloponnesian Wars against Athens, 431–404 B.C.

5. ATHENS

Athenian kingship abolished, ca. 683 B.C. Legal reforms of Solon instituted 594 B.C. Athens controlled Delian Confederacy—height of Athenian naval power, 454 B.C. Age of Pericles, 457–429 B.C.

6. GREAT AGE OF HELLAS, 490–338 B C.

Joint effort of the Greek city-states defeated the Persians at Marathon (490 B.C.) and Salamis (480 B.C.). Peloponnesian Wars (431–404 B.C.) weakened Greek city-states; Athens never fully recovered from losses. Conquest of Greek city-states by Philip II of Macedon at Battle of Chaeronea (338 B.C.) marked end of Hellenic independence and beginning of Greek absorption into Hellenistic civilization.

7. MAJOR FIGURES OF GREEK CIVILIZATION

a. Philosophers. (1) Sophists, fifth century B.C., believed that "man is the measure of all things"—i.e., that truth is what human beings think it is. This relativist position was attacked by other Greek thinkers who argued that there was an objective divine knowledge above and beyond man's senses. (2) Socrates, ca. 470–399 B.C., was a native of Athens who, in his search for truth, developed the method known as the Socratic dialogue, a system of questions and answers intended to make men think about their fundamental beliefs. Socrates concluded that ethics was not a matter of habit but could be deduced rationally, that virtue was knowledge, and that ignorance was the root of moral evil. He was put to death for asking disconcerting questions, which his enemies claimed were undermining the morals of Athenian youth. (3) Plato, ca. 427–347 B.C., was the foremost pupil of Socrates, who carried on where his master left off. He believed that men can know the good rationally and that, knowing it, they can also do good. Plato taught that there is an ideal world that exists in perfection above and beyond the material world and that this ideal world, which man knows through his spiritual faculty, is the only real world. (4) Aristotle, 384–322 B.C., was a brilliant pupil of Plato and one of the world's great systematizers of human knowledge. He formulated the laws of thought (logic) and tools

larger population of noncitizens (perioeci) and slaves (helots), has been the prototype throughout history of the closed, caste-ridden, authoritarian society. Its citizens were devoted to the ideals of self-denial and discipline as laid down in a rigorous code that regulated every aspect of Spartan life. Athens, on the other hand, once it had deposed its hereditary kings and destroyed the power of its factious nobility, emerged in the fifth century B.C., and particularly in the Age of Pericles (457–429 B.C.), as the classic democracy of the ancient world. By modern standards its democratic practices were extremely limited, since the rights of citizens were not extended to the whole society. Nevertheless, it offered its people a great measure of opportunity for self-expression and intellectual development, which accounts for the great cultural achievements of Athens in the fifth and fourth centuries B.C.

Unhappily for Greek civilization, the polis as a form of government was both its greatest strength and its greatest weakness. Only once in all their history were the city-states of Hellas able to combine successfully against outside danger; that occurred when the Persian Kings, Darius and Xerxes, in successive invasion attempts (490 and 480 B.C.), were defeated by the concerted action of a Hellenic alliance headed by Athens and Sparta. After the final Persian defeat in 479 B.C. incessant rivalry among the city-states, aroused by the growth of Athenian seapower and imperial ambitions, led to a series of internal wars between two alliances under Athenian and Spartan domination. As a consequence of this long struggle, known as the Peloponnesian Wars (431–404 B.C.), Athens was defeated; though she later recovered some of her former greatness, her position was never so strong again.

The succeeding period from 404 to 323 B.C. was marked by the predominance first of Sparta and then of Thebes. During that time the Persians and later the kings of Macedon (a semibarbarian kingdom to the north) intrigued continuously to keep Hellas disunited. Their success in doing so finally made it possible for King Philip of Macedon (359–336 B.C.) to defeat the Greek city-states one at a time and thus unite all Greece under Macedonian domination. After Philip's death his son Alexander the Great (336–323 B.C.) embarked with Greek aid on a campaign of conquest, which culminated in the destruction of the Persian Empire and the formation of a new, short-lived empire stretching from Greece to the borders of India. With Alexander's death in 323 B.C. the classic age of Hellenic civilization reached an end and merged into the Hellenistic, a new and broader civilization that reached far beyond Hellas.

The Greek influence on Western civilization has been so great and so significant that no area of western cultural or intellectual activity

of intellectual analysis that are the basis of western philosophy. He classi-
fied and arranged various fields of knowledge, such as physics, biology,
politics.

b. Artists.   (1) Phidias, 500?–432 B.C., greatest of Greek sculptors, created
the statue of Athena in the Parthenon in Athens and the forty-foot figure of
Zeus at Olympia. (2) Praxiteles, fourth century B.C., created the Hellenic
masterpiece of sculpture depicting Hermes bearing the infant Dionysius,
the only work clearly identified and associated with his name.

c. Literary Figures.   (1) Homer, ca. 850 B.C. There has always been much
speculation about the identity of this poet. The *Iliad* and the *Odyssey*,
which are attributed to him, had an immense influence on later Greek literature and thought. (2) Hesiod, ca. 700 B.C., was a Boeotian farmer-poet
whose chief writings were *Works and Days* and the *Theogony*. The latter
work is the chief source for Greek myths and legends about the gods.
(3) Pindar, ca. 522–443 B.C. The lyrics of this Theban poet were considered
finest after those of Homer. (4) Herodotus, ca. 484–425 B.C., and Thucydides,
ca. 471–400 B.C. The writings of these two historians are generally considered the finest examples of Greek prose. Herodotus recounted the history
of the Persian Wars, and Thucydides described the Peloponnesian Wars.
(5) Aeschylus, 525–456 B.C., was the author of *Prometheus Bound*, which
deals with the theme of man's relations with the gods. (6) Aristophanes,
ca. 448–380 B.C., master of Greek comedy, wrote the *Frogs* and a number
of other plays; he was a harsh social critic whose plays satirized the decline
of post-Periclean Athens. (7) Sophocles, ca. 496–406 B.C., author of the
Oedipus trilogy, was a master of Greek tragedy who questioned the meaning of life. (8) Euripides, ca. 480–406 B.C., wrote the *Bacchus, Iphigenia in
Aulis*, and *Madness of Heracles*, in which he raised doubts about Greek
religious belief and the morality of the gods.

8. SUMMARY OF THE GREEK CONTRIBUTION TO WESTERN CIVILIZATION

(1) Quality of inquisitiveness; (2) concern with the whole of human existence, spiritual as well as material; (3) belief in the power of the human mind
(rationalism) to find answers to all important questions; (4) belief in the
harmony of the universe.

has been untouched by it. For centuries Greek standards of value in the arts and the characteristic Greek approach to intellectual problems were accepted almost slavishly by men who looked backward to the Greeks as beings superior to themselves. Even in our own day, when we have long rejected some of the specific answers given by the Greeks to the questions they asked about man and the universe, we must still admit that few have ever formulated those questions more acutely or profoundly than they did.

It was, in fact, the quality of inquisitiveness that made the Greek contribution to Western civilization so significant. The Greeks asked questions about almost everything, and they asked them in a very specific way. The Greek not only was concerned to speculate about the gods and man's behavior toward them; he was also concerned with all the complex things (phenomena) of his daily world. Unlike many other ancient peoples, who also developed elaborate systems of philosophy or theology, the Greeks were not content to rely entirely upon the divine, the mysterious, or the unknowable as the means of explaining the world in which they lived. They believed firmly in the power of man's mind to seek out explanations; and they also believed that all the complex, diverse phenomena of the everyday world were governed by underlying harmonious laws that could be fathomed by human reason. This assumption of an underlying order or harmony in nature, while it may have been overstressed by the Greeks, was to have a profound influence on the development of knowledge and thought in mathematics and the natural sciences (astronomy, chemistry, physics), where order and harmony must also be presupposed.

The Greeks were also curious about man's mental processes and the abstractions that take form as ideas. In their pursuit of philosophy they continually tried to relate ideas to common sense experience, even when, on occasion, their speculations seemed very remote from day-to-day living. The comprehensiveness of their thought and the magnitude of their intellectual achievement, particularly that of the three greatest of their thinkers—Socrates (ca. 470–399 B.C.), Plato (ca. 427–347 B.C.), and Aristotle (384–322 B.C.)—seem all the more remarkable when we remember that they had to originate techniques for dealing with such problems.

In the arts the Greeks were also pioneers. Greek drama was an expression of Greek thought about man and the world. The earliest of the great Hellenic tragedians, Aeschylus (525–456 B.C.) and Sophocles (ca. 496–406 B.C.), presented in their dramas a kind of universal picture of those concepts about mankind that everyone accepted and that seemed to demonstrate that there was a moral order in the universe.

B. THE HELLENISTIC AGE, ca. 323–30 B.C.

1. CAREER OF ALEXANDER THE GREAT 336–323 B.C.

Succeeded his father, Philip II of Macedon, in 336 B.C.; crushed revolt of Greek city-states, 335; invaded the Persian Empire—battle of Granicus, 334; battle of Issus, 333; battle of Gaugamela (Arbela), 331; at the death of Darius, Alexander became Great King of Persia and extended his conquests to the banks of the Indus River in India.

2. DIVISION OF ALEXANDER'S EMPIRE, 321-301 B.C.

Ptolemy Soter seized Egypt 321; civil war (Wars of the Diadochi) waged

With the coming of Euripides (480–406 B.C.), the form of the drama changed, for Euripides raised questions about the relations of man with the gods and made it clear that he had serious doubts about the meaning and purpose of the universe as set forth in the older plays. The world, he noted, was not a place where morality inevitably triumphed. In this way, Euripides opened the door to new speculation about the goals of human existence and helped to prepare the way for a fully developed philosophy. For many Greeks this new philosophy gradually replaced the older religious faith in the gods. In spite of this great change, the Greeks never entirely gave up trying to portray through art certain generalized concepts that were a part of the earlier tradition. Architecture and sculpture, for example, usually demonstrated the harmony of soul and body as well as the Greek notion of balance or moderation in all things (*sophrosyne*). The most splendid examples of this artistic expression may be seen in the creations of Athenian artists during the sixth and fifth centuries B.C.

It is arguable whether the Greeks "invented" the notion that the world was governed by laws that took the form of logic and mathematics. For centuries men have tended to believe that the Greek faith in the rationality of the universe (i.e., that there is a cosmic order governed by laws that can be discovered by human reason, *see* pp. 7–8) was as "true" as anything in the world of human observation and experience could be. The faith in a rational universe has been and remains so fundamental a proposition of modern thought that, whether ultimately "true" or not, much of our philosophy and most of our scientific inquiry are founded upon it. If it is not "true," it remains one of the most useful and valuable myths, whose abolition would require rejection or reexamination of Western man's most basic precepts.

B. THE HELLENISTIC AGE

The Hellenistic Age lasted from the death of Alexander until the absorption of the whole eastern Mediterranean into the Roman Empire sometime around the beginning of the Christian Era. It was characterized by (1) the decline of the Greek city-state, (2) the diffusion of Greek culture throughout the ancient world, and (3) the steady progress of Roman conquest.

Following Alexander's death in 323 B.C., the greater part of his vast empire was fought over (Wars of the Diadochi) and finally divided among his generals. In the early third century B.C. these divisions consisted of Egypt (with Palestine and Phoenicia), ruled by Ptolemy; the

among Alexander's generals, 322–301. Battle of Ipsus, 301 B.C., settled final division of Alexander's kingdom.

3. HELLENISTIC AGE IN GREECE

Formation of the Aetolian (290 B.C.) and Achaean (280 B.C.) leagues. Philip V of Macedonia began hostilities with Rome, 215 B.C. Rome made Greek states into dependencies, 146 B.C.

4. HELLENISTIC AGE IN ASIA

Seleucus I founded Seleucid Empire, 305–280 B.C. Antiochus III defeated by Romans at Magnesia, 190 B.C. Independent kingdom of Pergamum bequeathed to Rome by its last king, 133 B.C. Syria and the remaining lands of the Seleucid Empire made a Roman province, 64 B.C.

5. HELLENISTIC AGE IN EGYPT

Egypt ruled by the descendants of Ptolemy Soter. Romans intervened (168 B.C.) to save Egypt from conquest by Syria (Seleucid Empire). Egypt became a Roman province at the defeat of Marc Antony and Cleopatra in the battle of Actium, 31 B.C.

6. CULTURAL ACHIEVEMENTS OF THE HELLENISTIC AGE

a. Philosophies. (1) Epicureanism was founded by Epicurus, an Athenian (ca. 342–270 B.C.), who taught that all human life was subservient to the pursuit of happiness. He believed, however, that it was best to cultivate the virtues rather than the vices because the latter, if pursued too much, usually caused pain and suffering. Epicurus thought of the universe as consisting of matter made up of atoms; the gods were remote from men; and religion was superstition. His greatest disciple was the Roman philosopher Lucretius (ca. 96–55 B.C.) whose long poem *De Rerum Natura (On the Nature of Things)* set forth the Epicurean philosophy in full. (2) Stoicism was founded by Zeno of Citium (336–264 B.C.). Though it took various forms, Stoicism in general taught that the world was ruled by a divine universal reason in which all mankind shared and that all men were members of a universal brotherhood. The duty of the Stoic was to live according to divine reason and, by cultivating the highest moral virtues, remain indifferent to the external things of this world. Thus he would achieve the true happiness that comes with serenity of mind. (3) Skepticism was founded by the half-legendary Pyrrho of Elis (ca. 360–ca. 270 B.C.). In essence, it was a philosophy that criticized all other philosophies. Skepticism denied that any knowledge was possible because all sense of perceptions are illusions. Therefore, man can know nothing with any certainty. All that he can hope to do is to accept the world as it is and maintain a complete calm in the face of life.

former Persian Empire, ruled by Seleucus; Macedonia; and the semi-independent Achaean and Aetolian confederacies, which comprised the former city-states of Greece. Most of these new states took on the characteristics of despotism as their rulers increasingly claimed for themselves a quasi-divine authority. Successor and fragmented states arose and quarreled. Continuous warfare during the third and second centuries B.C., however, finally brought on Roman intervention in the eastern Mediterranean and thus gradually diminished the independence of the Hellenistic states. By 30 B.C. all had become a part of the Roman Empire.

The culture of the Hellenistic Age was marked by two tendencies: cosmopolitanism, resulting from the disintegration of the city-state and the diffusion of Greek civilization; and individualism, seemingly caused by the breakdown of older religious loyalties and the disappearance of faith in the polis as the center of all human activity. These developments were accompanied by a growth of trade and finance, which enormously increased the wealth of the ancient world. As a result of these changes, new philosophical systems, largely secular in outlook, displaced older modes of thought. Man came to be looked upon as a being essentially interested in the things of this world who needed the guidance of a secularized code of ethics. This guidance the three major philosophical systems of the period (Epicureanism, Stoicism, and Skepticism) sought to give, stressing self-discipline and equanimity in the face of adverse circumstances. Perhaps the greatest achievements of the Hellenistic Age, however, were in the sciences. Euclid and Archimedes in mathematics; Heracleides, Aristarchus, and Hipparchus in astronomy; Eratosthenes in geography; and Herophilus and Erasistratus in medicine—all made contributions of permanent importance in the history of scientific knowledge.

Certain fundamental changes within the Hellenistic world prepared the way for the ultimate absorption of all the states that succeeded the Alexandrian conquest into the Roman system of imperial administration. One important reason for these changes was that the original Greek communities, while they exported their ideas and culture to Asia and Egypt, were also influenced by those regions. Throughout the Mediterranean East during the Hellenistic period Greek ways and ideas were accepted and imitated. Upper-class Persians, Anatolians, and Egyptians immersed themselves in Greek culture and used the Greek language as a kind of universal language for the conduct of commercial life and administration.

The very success of this Greek cultural expansion, however, had serious consequences for the original communities of the Greek main-

b. Scientific Achievements.   (1) Mathematics. Euclid (ca. 300 B.C.), greatest of Greek geometers, collected all the works of his predecessors and gave to geometry the form it has taken since. Archimedes of Syracuse (287?–212 B.C.) discovered the idea of specific gravity, worked out the principle of the lever, and found the ratio of the volume of a cylinder to that of a sphere inscribed within it. (2) Astronomy. Heracleides of Pontus (fourth century B.C.) about 350 B.C. maintained in his history of astronomy that the earth rotated on its axis and that Venus and Mercury revolved around the sun. Aristarchus of Samos (third century B.C.) went further and found by geometry that the sun was larger than the earth; also asserted that the earth moved around the sun. Hipparchus of Nicea (ca. 130 B.C.) cleared up the mathematical difficulties in the geocentric (earth-centered) theory of the solar system so that it became the accepted theory until Copernicus disproved it mathematically in the sixteenth century. (3) Geography, Eratosthenes (third century B.C.) calculated the diameter of the earth with only a small margin of error; computed the distance from the earth to the sun with an error of only one percent; produced a map with lines of latitude and longitude. (4) Medicine. Herophilus (ca. 300 B.C.) was the first known to have undertaken anatomical dissection. Erasistratus (ca. 300 B.C.), pupil of Herophilus, is generally regarded as the founder of physiology.

A frequent question about the Hellenistic Age is why the scientific and technological achievements of the period did not lead to something like an "industrial" or "scientific revolution," which might have transformed the ancient Mediterranean world and preserved the continuity of its civilization. The answer is that isolated creative acts or discoveries cannot have far-reaching effects unless the society in which they occur has developed mass literacy and capital accumulation and a large labor force ready to make use of them. These elements were not present in the Hellenistic world, nor would any society have them in sufficiency for many centuries to come.

land. If the Oriental was increasingly Hellenized, Greece itself was also assimilating Oriental ways. Whatever the reason (and we are still not sure why the change occurred), Greek society became more and more Oriental in form and structure, particularly in its economic life. The large estate worked by numbers of slaves or wage-earning laborers displaced the independent small farmer. Cities were populated by a proletariat whose members suffered dreadfully from sudden shifts in economic circumstances. Even worse, because most of the larger Greek cities depended on food from abroad, any crop failure or interruption of supply could produce serious famines. The result was a continuously growing discontent in most Greek cities, which occasionally reached the point of riot or rebellion. Moreover, the growing gap between rich and poor increased class bitterness and further weakened the structure of society.

The great and basic problem of this period, as it was to be of the Roman Empire in its later stages, was that the growth of urbanization had, in many ways, outstripped the technology of the times. The methods of production then available simply were not advanced enough to support the dense city populations of the Hellenistic world. The result was that the insufficiency of wealth produced further tensions by making it very nearly impossible to alleviate the lot of the great mass of the poverty-stricken population.

A further consequence of this situation was the destruction of the old loyalties that had bound the city-state communities of Hellas together. Most Hellenistic cities, therefore, lived in constant danger of social explosion, a situation that in the end must have aided the Roman conquest of the eastern Mediterranean.

To add to the social difficulties of the Hellenistic world, the traditional religious beliefs no longer appealed to the upper classes. In their place the cultivated rich substituted the secular philosophies mentioned above. These, while satisfactory under normal human conditions, had no great sustaining power in times of crisis. For the masses, on the other hand, a secularized code of ethics not only was remote from their own understanding and experiences but seemed, in fact, only to suggest that they should accept their sufferings with a resigned hopelessness. It is not surprising, therefore, that a whole host of mystery cults should have been recreated (as in the case of the Greek mystery religions) or newly founded. An interesting example of the latter was the worship of Serapis. Serapis, the city god of Alexandria in Egypt, appears to have been a deliberate invention that grew out of a combination of older deities: the Egyptian god Osiris, the Greek Zeus, and the Babylonian Marduk. The cult had the great advantage of offering im-

C. ROME: REPUBLIC AND EMPIRE, ca. 509 B.C.–A.D. 476

1. THE ROMAN REPUBLIC, ca. 509 B.C.–27 B.C.

a. Early History of the City. Growth of the power of the masses (plebeians) characterized the early history of Rome. Expulsion of Roman kings, ca. 509 B.C. (1) Law of the Twelve Tables formulated as the basis of all later Roman law, 450–449 B.C. Consulship opened to plebeians, 367 B.C. (2) Reforms of the Gracchi (Tiberius Gracchus, murdered in 133 B.C., and his brother Gaius Gracchus, killed in 121 B.C.) attempted to redistribute land and wealth in favor of the Roman masses.

b. Civil Wars of the First Century B.C. Internal disturbances led to a series of dictatorships, sometimes favoring the aristocracy and sometimes favoring the plebeians. Despite efforts of various powerful leaders— Marius, Sulla, Pompey, and, finally, Julius Caesar—to restore order, none could do so successfully until Octavius (Augustus) Caesar suppressed the warring factions and seized power in 27 B.C. By this action the Roman Republic ceased to exist and was gradually transformed into a centralized empire.

mortality to those who observed its rituals, a characteristic that may well explain its spread throughout the Hellenistic world.

In spite of all its extraordinary achievements in science, technology, and the arts, Hellenistic society was slowly losing its creative impulses in the generations just before its conquest by the Romans. The age was one that seems in retrospect to have promised much but that could not continuously sustain the high intellectual and artistic effort of the earlier Hellenic civilization from whence it sprang.

C. ROME: REPUBLIC AND EMPIRE

From the point of view of Western man, ancient history culminates with the absorption of the whole Mediterranean basin into the single great political entity known as the Roman Empire. The history of this great empire, which so influenced world history, divides into two obvious parts. The first period, that of the Roman Republic, lasted from about 509 B.C., when the Romans expelled the last of their early kings, to 27 B.C., when Augustus (27 B.C.–A.D. 14), emerged as the first Roman emperor. The second, or imperial, period extended from the reign of Augustus to the end of the Roman Empire in the West toward the end of the fifth century A.D.

The story of Rome is one of a fairly steady and almost uninterrupted expansion during which a small hill town near the mouth of the Tiber River in west central Italy became the great urban center of a vast empire that encircled the Mediterranean and ultimately included all or parts of modern England, France, Germany, and Spain. This growth was the result not of any carefully conceived plan but of a need, first, to defend the city itself and, later, to protect the distant frontiers of regions that Roman conquest had added over a long period of time. In this fashion, Roman conquests compounded themselves; for, as the territories of Rome grew, other more distant peoples continually threatened Roman security. In the end, this continuous expansion forced the city to become an imperial power and drove the Romans to change their quasi-democratic republican institutions in order to set up a system of government that could more effectively deal with the complex administrative problems of a great empire.

In its early stages (before 31 B.C.) this expansion was marked by several important wars of survival and conquest. Defeating first their immediate neighbors, the Etruscans, the Romans gradually extended their territory, until by 265 B.C. all Italy was conquered. With Italy secured, Rome then found herself involved in a series of fateful wars

c. Expansion of the Roman Republic, 388–31 B.C.   Rome defeated Latin League, 388 B.C.; conquered the Samnites, 327–290 B.C.; defeated Pyrrhus of Epirus and seized Magna Graecia (southern Italy), 281–272 B.C. First Punic War with Carthage, 264–241 B.C Sicily, Sardinia, and Corsica became first Roman provinces, 227 B.C. Second Punic War, 218–201 B.C., ended after defeat of Hannibal by the Roman general Scipio Africanus at the battle of Zama (Africa), 202 B.C. Third Punic War, 149–146 B.C., led to the ruthless destruction of Carthage. Macedonia became a Roman province, 146 B.C. Conquest and reorganization of Asia by Pompey, 66–62 B.C. Caesar's conquest of Gaul, 58–51 B.C. Egypt became a Roman province, 31 B.C.

2. THE ROMAN EMPIRE, 27 B.C.–A.D. 476

a. The Early Empire, 27 B.C.–A.D. 180   Augustus Caesar granted imperial power for life, 23 B.C. Roman armies under Varus defeated by Germans (battle of Teutoburger Forest), A.D. 9. Imperial expansion continued under Tiberius, A.D. 14–37, Caligula, A.D. 37–41, Claudius, A.D. 41–54 (under whom Romans began conquest of British in A.D. 43), and Nero, A.D. 54–68. Empire reached its greatest extent under the "five good emperors": Nerva, A.D. 96–98, Trajan, A.D. 98–117, Hadrian, A.D. 117–138, Antoninus Pius, A.D. 138–161, and Marcus Aurelius (whose *Meditations* made him famous also as a philosopher), A.D. 161–180.

b. The Later Empire, A.D. 180–476.   After A.D. 180 the forces of disintegration were clearly at work. The empire was increasingly controlled by military factions, which deposed and often murdered emperors. The state was no longer able to maintain its extended frontiers or to preserve internal order. Gradually, the machinery of government ceased to function with its former effectiveness. Taxes became more difficult to collect, and the productive capacity of the empire declined. "Barrack emperors" ruled the empire with the support of the army, 235–284. Two emperors appointed to rule, 293.

Growing Christian minority persecuted, 303–311. Empire divided under eastern and western emperors, 305; permanent division of the empire began. Imperial order gave to Christianity equal rights with all other religions of the empire, 313. Founding of Constantinople as capital of Eastern Empire by Emperor Constantine, 330. Constantine's conversion to Christianity and death, 337. Invading Goths defeated imperial armies at Adrianople, 378. Sack of Rome by Alaric and the Visigoths, 410. Romans defeated the invading Huns under Attila at the battle of Chalons, 451. Sack of Rome by Gaeseric and the Vandals, 455. Odoacer, a Latinized German in command of the Roman armies, deposed the last western emperor (Romulus Augustulus) and ruled as a separate, independent king in Italy, 476.

with the North African state of Carthage. In three separate struggles known as the Punic Wars (264–241 B.C., 218–202 B.C., and 149–146 B.C.), Rome destroyed Carthage completely and converted Carthaginian territories into Roman provinces. During the second of these wars Rome first turned her attention to the East, where Philip V, king of Macedonia, had allied himself with the famous Carthaginian general Hannibal and started to war against Rome, setting in motion the train of events leading to Roman conquest of Greece and the Near East.

With the last of these conquests Rome herself began to change. Gradually the city expanded in wealth and population until it became a huge dependent urban growth whose subsistence was derived from outlying areas and whose social structure was altered in such a way as to create tensions among the various classes. During most of the first century B.C. Rome was torn by civil wars and social strife, which usually centered round the dictatorial chiefs of powerful factions. The greatest of these was Julius Caesar, who was murdered by his political enemies in 44 B.C. In the end, it was a young relative of Caesar's, Octavian (Augustus), who restored order by suppressing the various warring elements and making himself the first of the Roman emperors.

Under Augustus and his successors, imperial Rome reached the peak of its wealth and greatness as the central power of the state was increasingly consolidated around the person of the emperor and as the boundaries of the empire were steadily expanded. By A.D. 117 the empire reached its broadest extent, but even as it grew there were already signs of decay. The cost of maintaining large military forces; the continuing economic dependence of the capital city upon the provinces; the increasing insecurity of the emperors, who depended more and more upon the army to keep them in power; the inability of the empire to absorb large numbers of infiltrating barbarians—all helped to weaken the central authority and undermine the social structure. In their desperation the later emperors resorted to repressive measures in the form of harsh taxation and economic regulation, which slowly strangled economic activity and thus further compounded the difficulties of the state. Meanwhile, Christianity, which had been introduced into Rome from the Near East during the first century A.D., gradually spread throughout the empire. At the opening of the fourth century (ca. 313) it was granted equal status with the older pagan religions on orders of Emperor Constantine. In the end, the various forces of disintegration led to the deposition of the last western emperor (as distinct from the eastern emperor who, after the division of the empire into two parts in 395, ruled the eastern half from Constantinople) and his replacement by a barbarian king. With this event the real unity of the

3. MAJOR FIGURES OF ROMAN CIVILIZATION

a. **Statesmen and Military Leaders.**   (1) Scipio Africanus, 237–183 B.C.
Defeated Hannibal and the Carthaginian army at the battle of Zama (Africa),
202 B.C. (2) Marcus Porcius Cato ("the Censor"), 234–149 B.C. Roman
senator and chief of the landowning party who demanded the destruction
of Carthage in the Third Punic War by insisting *"delenda est Carthago"*
(Carthage must be destroyed). (3) Gnaeus Pompey, 106–48 B.C. Conqueror
of Syria and Roman Asia; ruled Rome as a part of a triumvirate (three-man
dictatorship) with Crassus and Julius Caesar (who was his son-in-law);
became sole dictator in 52 B.C. and was finally defeated by Julius Caesar at
the battle of Pharsalus, 48 B.C. (4) Julius Caesar, ca 100–44 B.C. Conqueror
of Gaul; member of triumvirate with Pompey; after his victory at Pharsalus
became virtually an absolute dictator. From fear that he was about to
establish some kind of permanent monarchy, he was assassinated by a band
of plotters led by Marcus Junius Brutus in 44 B.C. (5) Marcus Antonius
(Marc Antony), ca. 83–30 B.C. Associate of Julius Caesar who later divided
power with Octavius (Augustus) Caesar. He fell under the influence of and
later married Cleopatra of Egypt. When he tried to dispose of Rome's
eastern provinces in her favor, he was defeated by Augustus at Actium in
31 B.C. and afterwards took his own life. (6) Augustus Caesar (Octavius or
Octavianus), 63 B.C.–A.D. 14. Greatnephew and adopted heir of Julius
Caesar; restored order in Roman provinces and became first Roman emperor (princeps), 27 B.C.–A.D. 14. (7) Trajan (Marcus Ulpius Traianus),
ca. A.D. 52–117. Usually thought of as the greatest emperor after Augustus;
excellent soldier; able administrator; expanded the empire to its greatest
territorial extent; ruled from A.D. 98 to 117. (8) Marcus Aurelius (Antonius),
A.D. 121–180. Last of the "five good emperors"; able soldier and administrator; preserved the empire from invasion; Stoic philosopher whose
Meditations have a Christian flavor. (9) Diocletian, A.D. 245–313. Emperor

Roman empire was destroyed. In its place appeared the numerous German tribal principalities that became the bases of modern European nationhood.

The most important contributions of the Roman world to later western history is to be found in its bringing together of the various streams of ancient civilization and its transmission of these to the European successor states. Though the Romans added to Greek thought little that was original (they were particularly deficient in science and philosophy), they were enough impressed by it to act as its disseminators. For the spread of Christianity they provided a stable political setting and an institutional framework that was copied by the Christian church and enabled the church to grow in strength through the centuries. To the world of European literature and thought the Romans bequeathed their Latin language, which was to become an influential element in the formation of almost every western European tongue. Of equal importance were Rome's laws and her system of universal government, from both of which many of the later political institutions of Europe were derived.

Historical Problem of Rome's Decline. The reason for the long decline and ultimate disappearance of the Roman Empire of the West has long stirred the imagination of historians. Historians are always curious about the reasons why any great civilization disappears. In the case of the Western Roman Empire, however, curiosity is compounded by the fact that the empire lasted for so many centuries and seemed, both to contemporaries and to later generations, to be one of the most stable and longest-lived political entities ever created. Its disintegration, therefore, seemed to those who witnessed the last days of the Roman Empire to be the end of the world. Indeed, it was this very sense of secular hopelessness that the great Christian thinker, Augustine (A.D. 356–430), sought to combat in a famous work entitled *The City of God.* Augustine argued that while the "City of Man"—i.e., Rome—might well fade from history, men should still be of good hope. The "City of God"—i.e., Christianity—would take its place, and men might therefore be consoled by the hope of a kingdom that was not of this world.

Nevertheless, though the views of Augustine and other Christian theologians offered consolation to faithful Christian believers, other Romans thought the decline of the empire a disaster and undertook to explain it in various ways. Even so early as the end of the first century A.D. the Roman historian Tacitus (ca. A.D. 55—ca. 117) suggested that the decline of older republican virtues, particularly in the army,

who restored order after a period of anarchy ("crisis of the third century") and instituted a series of reforms that, for a time, stopped the decay of the Roman state. Remembered for his persecution of Christians. Came to the throne in 284; abdicated in 305. (10) Constantine the Great, ca. A.D. 280–337. Successor of Diocletian; established Christianity on equal footing with other religions and later made it the state religion; converted the empire into a hereditary monarchy. Ruled from 305 to 337. (11) Justinian, A.D. 483–565. Emperor of the East (527–565) who almost succeeded in reunifying the eastern and western halves of the empire by conquest. His most enduring work was the collection and codification of the Roman law, which has come down in history as the Code of Justinian.

b. Major Figures of Roman Culture. (1) Cicero, 106–43 B.C. Greatest of Roman rhetoricians (orators), whose speeches and writings proved hm one of the great masters of the Latin language. (2) The Roman Historians. Livy, 59 B.C.–A.D. 17, in his *History of Rome* described the beginnings of the city and the origins of Roman greatness to a later generation. Tacitus (ca. 55 to after A.D. 117) in his *Annals and Histories*, strove to demonstrate to the Romans of his day how decadent they had become. (3) Vergil (or Virgil), 70–19 B.C. Greatest Roman epic poet; author of the *Aeneid*, which tells at length the story of Rome's founding by the legendary Aeneas of Troy. (4) Ovid, 43 B.C.–ca. A.D. 17. Author of a handbook of Greek mythology known as the *Metamorphoses* and numerous witty poems. (5) Two Roman Satirists. Satire in its pure form was an original contribution of the Romans to western literature. Its first major practitioner was Horace, 65–8 B.C., whose *Odes* made him the second greatest of the Latin poets (after Vergil). The greatest of Roman satirists, however, was Juvenal, A.D., 60?–140?, whose *Satires* still give a harsh but shrewd and subtle picture of Roman life.

led to a moral decay that rotted the empire from within. Some emperors of the third and fourth centuries, most notably Julian the Apostate, who ruled from 361 to 363, tried to restore the old pagan religion in the hope that this might revive the ancient virtues.

Much later in European history historians came to share a widely held view that the Roman Empire was destroyed by invading hordes of barbarians (Huns, Ostrogoths, Visigoths, Vandals) who poured over the imperial frontiers in such numbers that they could not be resisted. The flood of these uncivilized warriors was so great, they believed, that it inundated Roman civilization and ushered in the long period known as "the Dark Ages," from which Europe did not begin to recover for almost a thousand years. The great shortcoming of this overly simple explanation was that it overlooked one very important consideration. Rome had been threatened by outside enemies time after time throughout its history. On countless previous occasions, Roman armies had thrown the invaders back or conquered and enslaved them.

Why were the Romans of the later period (fourth and fifth centuries) unable to do what Romans of earlier periods had done so often and so effectively? The answer to this question began to be pondered by historians from about the eighteenth century onward. One of the first modern historians to think about this question at length was the great British scholar, Edward Gibbon (1737–1794), whose many-volume *Decline and Fall of the Roman Empire* remains one of the classics of historical writing even to this day. Gibbon concluded that if the later Romans were unable to resist barbarian incursions, it was not because the barbarians were numerically stronger or more warlike than earlier invaders. On the contrary, it seemed obvious to Gibbon, as it had to some Roman observers, that something had happened to the Romans themselves that made them less successful in resisting outside assault. Gibbon implied that a partial explanation might be found in the emergence of Christianity, which weakened the warlike spirit of the Romans.

Gibbon's views in this connection are no longer widely accepted by scholars. Nevertheless, most contemporary historians would agree that the "fall of the Roman Empire" came about as a result of internal causes. At present, while there is still a great deal of varied scholarly opinion on the subject, the most widely held views might be summarized as follows: (1) the empire collapsed for a combination of economic and social reasons; (2) the most important of these was the growth of the city of Rome, whose huge population had to be supported at the expense of the provinces; (3) the empire failed to improve its (techno-

4. SUMMARY OF THE ROMAN CONTRIBUTION TO WESTERN CIVILIZATION

(1) Transmission of the traditions and learning of the ancient world; (2) stable political framework for the growth of Christianity; (3) Latin language and literature; (4) Roman law and government.

logical) productive capacities above the level of a slave economy; and (4) the church in the later empire was unable to solve the problem of Christian heresies, whose adherents, particularly in North Africa, became permanent dissenters from imperial authority.

chapter five

EVENTS AND DEFINITIONS

In the centuries between A.D. 500 and 1000 the geographical region known of Europe took on distinct cultural and political characteristics that would separate it historically from the ancient civilizations of the Mediterranean region. As a result of this separation, the core region of the West—consisting of the kingdoms and states that evolved out of the barbarian Germanic kingdoms that superseded the Roman Empire—would come into existence about the end of the first millennium A.D. At that time the core region would be known as Latin Christendom (after the western or Latin church centered at Rome), or simply Christendom to its inhabitants. Later, Christendom itself would evolve into the secular civilization that has been known as Europe during the past several centuries.

The forces that helped to form Europe were many and complex, but three were more significant than all the others: (1) the Christian tradition; (2) the Latin church, which set an institutional example for the feudal monarchies that later evolved into the national states of early modern Europe; and (3) the Germanic peoples whose warbands conquered the original areas of the later national states. Out of the fusion of these elements came Europe and, in time, Western civilization.

The Making of
Europe, 500-1000

In modern times it has been customary to think of Europe as a separate geographic entity, a continent distinct from the other continental land masses of the earth. In fact, Europe is separated not geographically but culturally from Asia and Africa; even in cultural terms it is not always easy to determine Europe's boundaries, since so much of European civilization has been derived from or overlapped into Asia and Africa. For purposes of definition most historians now think of Europe as the creation of a Latin western culture fostered and spread by the medieval Latin church. In this sense Europe does possess a measure of cultural unity that, in all its essentials, was formed in the period extending from the end of the fifth century A.D. to the beginning of the eleventh century A.D. The three prominent characteristics of this period are (1) the superseding of the urban civilization of Rome by an agrarian society whose economic structure was based upon the great estate or manor and whose political organization was determined by the personal-contractual relations of feudalism; (2) the development of the western church under the headship of the Roman pontiff (pope) to a point where, in the twelfth and thirteenth centuries, it became a suprana-

A. THE CHRISTIAN FOUNDATIONS

1. THE ORIGINS OF CHRISTIANITY

a. Greek Sources.   Decline of the traditional Greek religions during the Hellenistic Age left many Greeks without any belief that transcended their daily lives. Secular or vaguely religious philosophies like Epicureanism, Stoicism, and Skepticism were not enough to fill the void, particularly for the masses. Thus there occurred during the period of Roman rule a gradual revival of interest in religion and religious ceremonies, especially those originating in the Orient. One of these eastern religions, Christianity, soon transcended all others in importance and began to spread rapidly through the Greek portions of the empire from the end of the first century A.D.

b. Jewish Sources.   Growth of a strong and traditional Messianic feeling (belief in the imminent coming of a Messiah or savior) among the Jews of the first century B.C. and the later infiltration of Greek ideas into Jewish thought prepared the way for the acceptance of Christianity.

c. Life of Christ.   Recounted in the four gospels according to Matthew, Mark, Luke, and John. Birth of Jesus Christ at Bethlehem in Judaea, ca. 4 B.C. Mission and preaching of Christ, ca. A.D. 26–30. Crucifixion, ca. A.D. 30.

d. Teachings of Jesus Christ.   It should be remembered that an important part of the teaching of Jesus was through the example of his own life, since his acts as well as his words had a great impact on those who knew him or were told about him. In the main his teachings were simple: true religion comes from the heart; and all the law and the prophets' teachings depend on two commandments—love God and love thy neighbor.

e. Universality of Christian Appeal.   An important aspect of these teachings was that they appealed to men in all stations of life, and particularly to the humble masses throughout the empire. Christianity in its primitive form offered a hope to those whose lot in life was an unhappy one.

2. THE SPREAD OF CHRISTIANITY

The appeal of Christian teaching and the story of Christ's resurrection quickly gave the new religion a following among the Jews, but it was not until the conversion of the Hellenized Jew, Saul of Tarsus (afterwards known

tional institution of great moral power and authority; and (3) the beginnings of a conception of unified political authority under the rule of the feudal king that, in time, was to lead to the development of the modern national state.

A. THE CHRISTIAN FOUNDATIONS

It is important to remember that medieval civilization was profoundly Christian in the sense that Christian beliefs and standards, though sometimes imperfectly realized, were the bases of thought and the molders of tradition. Christ was the divine redeemer of mankind who had provided the means by which all men, whatever their race or social condition, might hope to achieve a life immortal. In the view of medieval man, the means of attaining this end had been given by Christ to his apostles and thus to the Christian church. Hence the church's duty was to preserve the faith and orthodoxy of those who already believed and to strive to win over those who did not. This strong sense of obligation, which was first put into practice by St. Paul, the "apostle to the gentiles," in the first century A.D., made Christianity a powerful missionary religion and led during the early Middle Ages (sixth through tenth centuries) to its expansion into northern and western Europe. As its missionaries spread the faith, the church everywhere adapted itself to a variety of social conditions and imparted through its institutions not only the ethics and beliefs of Christianity but also certain of the traditions of classical antiquity that had been made a part of Christian teaching by the fathers of the church. Apart, however, from its ethical and cultural influences, the Latin church also had an important secular effect on the life of medieval man. Through the machinery of an international bureaucracy and by its dissemination of the Roman law, the church became the teacher of the feudal monarchies, which quickly adapted the practices of ecclesiastical administration to serve their own ends. By means, too, of the great monastic orders (originating in the East but transferred to the West by Benedict of Nursia in the sixth century), techniques and skills of various kinds were developed and spread through societies where they would otherwise have been unknown. The medieval Latin church thus evolved into a massive international organization whose spiritual head, the pope, possessed enormous temporal as well as ecclesiastical power.

Perhaps more important for the larger development of Western civilization, however, was the body of practices and ideas that came into being within the community of western Latin Christianity—i.e., that body of Christian communicants who over the centuries looked to

to Christians as St. Paul), that Christianity began to win converts extensively outside Judaic circles.

a.   Work of Paul, ca. A.D. 34–60.   Paul, a Roman citizen who was learned in the Greek language and literature, was able to speak to the Roman world in a widely understood tongue; he also elaborated the first Christian theology in attempting to explain the new faith. Paul pressed the view that non-Jews (gentiles) need not become Jews or observe the Hebraic religious laws in order to become Christians but needed only to have faith in Christ. In this way Christianity ceased to be a sect of Judaism and became a separate universal religion.

b.   Christianization of the Roman Empire, A.D. 64–455.   Fire of Rome and massacre of Christians under Nero, A.D. 64. Rescript of Marcus Aurelius against Christians, 169. Persecutions by Emperor Decius, 249–251. General toleration granted to Christians by Constantine and the Eastern emperor Licinius (Edict of Milan), 313. Council of Nicea defined the doctrine of the Trinity for orthodox Christian belief, 325. Conversion and death of Constantine, 337. Western bishops subjugated to Pope Leo I by order of Emperor Valentinian III (supremacy of Roman bishops), 455.

c.   Rise of Monasticism and the Spread of Christianity to Northern and Western Europe, ca. 360–1000.   (1) Monasticism, the ascetic practice of living apart from the world of men, did not originate with Christianity but came to be associated with it at a very early period in the Christian communities of Syria and Egypt, where it was well established in the third and fourth centuries. It was carried to the West about the middle of the fourth century and there was given the form of a corporate community (all monks lived together in a monastery) by St. Benedict of Nursia in 529. According to St. Benedict's rule (on which all later monastic rules were founded), it was the monk's duty to do the "work of God"—praying, fasting, performing the rites of the church, working with his hands (and, later, with his brains). Traveling as lone missionaries or in groups, the Christian monks of the early Middle Ages were important in the spread of Christianity throughout northern and western Europe. (2) Spread of Christianity to northern and western Europe. St. Patrick's mission to Ireland, ca. 431; beginning of a separate Celtic church. St. Columba, an Irish monk, carried Christianity into Scotland, 563. St. Augustine of Canterbury reintroduced Christianity into England, 597. Irish (Celtic) church submitted to the Latin Catholic (Roman) church at Synod of Whitby, 664. Mission of the English monk St. Boniface (Winfred) established the Latin church in Germany, 722–754. Conversion of Scandinavia (Denmark, Norway, Sweden), ca. 950–1000.

the Roman pontiffs for spiritual leadership. Indeed, the Latin Christian tradition was to be of such significance in the development of later Western civilization that it would be impossible to enumerate all or even most of its major contributions in brief space. Nevertheless, some are of such transcendent importance that they must be mentioned here.

As the Roman Empire itself had been the means by which much of the civilization of antiquity was transmitted to Europe and the West, so too was Latin Christianity. The Latin church was, after all, an institutional creation of the late Roman Empire. The center of its administrative authority was at Rome, and from a very early period the Roman bishops were generally acknowledged as heads of the church. Furthermore, the diocesan centers of ecclesiastical administration were usually situated in older centers of Roman imperial administration. Therefore, even after the empire itself had disappeared, the outline of its defunct system of government was preserved in the organization of the church. Thus the church continued to hope for a restoration of the lost imperial system that had nurtured it in its beginnings, and to strive throughout the early Middle Ages for a revival of strong Roman rule.

The church also kept alive the language of the empire. The Latin tongue, though it gradually underwent transformation during the immediate post-Roman and later medieval periods, remained the liturgical language that every cleric had to have some knowledge of in order to perform his ecclesiastical functions. In this way, as the church's influence spread into the remotest corners of Europe, later generations were provided with a key to at least part of the great artistic and intellectual treasury of classical civilization.

A continuing knowledge of the secular intellectual tradition of antiquity created a curious problem for Christianity, however, which was not finally to be resolved until the High Middle Ages. Early Christians were singularly indifferent to worldly things, including secular learning. They were convinced, first of all, that they were only sojourners in this world. Christ had seemed to imply in his conversations with his disciples that he would soon return to this earth and that this second coming would usher in the last days foretold by prophecy. Buoyed by this hope of imminent return, the earliest Christians tended to believe that any plans for the permanent existence of a Christian community in a secular world were vain and needless. As time passed, however, and the second coming became an ever remoter hope, the practices and attitudes of Christians began to change in two significant ways.

3. THE DEVELOPMENT OF CHRISTIAN THEOLOGY: THE EARLY FATHERS

As Christianity spread, it was confronted with the serious problem of determining what was the true or orthodox belief of Christians, particularly in view of the large number of variant interpretations given to Christ's teachings. One of the ways in which the early church dealt with this problem was by summoning great councils like the Council of Nicea (see p. 66), which defined orthodox belief on the nature of the Trinity in the Nicene Creed. With their increasing authority over the whole church, the Roman bishops (popes) successfully asserted their claim to adjudicate in matters of heresy; and councils were called with less frequency until they finally fell into abeyance. During these early centuries, however, the orthodox theology that both popes and councils preached was defined by a number of theologians who came to be known as "Fathers of the Church." Among the more famous of these fathers were those listed below.

a. Athanasius, ca. 293–373. Saint and bishop of Alexandria who attacked the Arian heresy (see below) by asserting the unity of God and the divinity of Christ.

b. Jerome, ca. 340–420. Translated the Bible from Greek and Hebrew sources into the Latin Vulgate edition, which became the standard for the western church.

c. John Chrysostom, ca. 345–407. Saint and patriarch of Constantinople (398–404); most influential of the Greek fathers; elevated asceticism in Christian practice and stressed the importance of scriptural study.

d. Augustine, 354–430. Saint and bishop of Hippo in North Africa; greatest of the Latin (western) fathers. Attacked the Pelagian or free-will heresy (see below) and laid stress on justification by faith. Prepared the way for the acceptance of Christian theology by the Germanic peoples of northern Europe. Augustine was a dominant force in Latin (western) theology throughout the early Middle Ages.

4. HERESIES

The following were some of the more troublesome of the heresies that divided the early church.

a. Arianism. Formulated by Arius of Alexandria early in the fourth century, Arianism tried to explain the relationship between Father and Son in the Trinity by saying that Christ, though possessing divine substance, was not coequal with God. This teaching was condemned by the Council of Nicea in 325 but persisted for some generations thereafter.

First, in order to preserve orthodoxy and to keep in communication with the everspreading branches of the Christian community, the church ceased to be a loose confederation of congregations and became an organically organized institution. With this transformation the early church began a pattern of development that later saw Christianity evolve into the most highly institutionalized of all the world's religions. The growth of this institutionalization was unquestionably of enormous importance for later periods of European and Western history. Not only did this development lead to the creation of one of the greatest supranational institutions the world has ever seen—that is, the medieval church—but it also provided for the continuous acquisition and augmentation of a body of administrative experience, which later enabled the church to act as the teacher of the medieval monarchy. Ultimately, then, it may be said that the church's institutional administrative experience contributed significantly to the formation of that other unique institutional creation of the Western world, the modern national state.

Second, once it was plain that Christianity would have to exist in the secular historical world for an unforeseeably long time, the church had to come to grips with certain of the secular intellectual influences by which it was surrounded. It was all well and good for ascetic Christians to preach that secular learning and philosophy were irrelevancies with which no true believer firmly fixed upon otherworldly goals should concern himself. But the writings and the philosophical speculations of the great pagans existed and could not be completely ignored. Indeed, as time passed and more and more intellectuals in late Roman society became Christian converts, it was virtually impossible for these men to completely forget the intellectual baggage they had accumulated before embracing the new faith. St. Augustine of Hippo is an excellent case in point. Augustine as a young man had been schooled in the pagan philosophies. When he became a Christian, he accepted the common Christian view that his earlier intellectual training was irrelevant to his new-found Christian aspirations. Yet he could not cast aside this knowledge or the ways of thought imparted by his pagan teachers. As he speculated about the relationship between the human and the divine, about God's grace and man's will, he inevitably used the familiar modes of thought. In brief, he speculated rationally on these matters even though he did not believe that reason alone could lead to faith. The important thing about him and generations of Christian thinkers like him was that they were creating that highly rationalized, highly sophisticated body of religious thought that we know as theology. Time after time in the history of the Christian church theo-

b. Gnosticism. This doctrine held that knowledge (*gnosis*) will liberate one from the physical (material) world, which is deemed only an illusion, the real world being that of the spirit.

c. Pelagianism. Named for the fourth-century British monk Pelagius, this doctrine argued that men were free of original sin and had control of their own moral destinies (free will). Condemned by Augustine and others because it lessened the divine power of God.

d. Nestorianism. Taught by Bishop Nestorius in the early fifth century, Nestorianism held that Christ was of two harmonious but distinct natures, human and divine. This belief led to a denial of the motherhood of the Virgin Mary and was condemned by the Council of Ephesus in 431.

e. Monophysitism. Arising particularly in Syrian and Egyptian Christianity, Monophysitism held that Christ was of one composite nature (not two as the Nestorians had taught) that was both human and divine. Its condemnation as a heresy by the Council of Chalcedon in 451 so angered its Syrian and Egyptian supporters that they later offered little resistance to Islamic (Mohammedan) conquest.

logians might protest that their speculations were vain, that men could never hope to come to a knowledge of God through reason alone. Yet they continually yielded to intellectual temptation. Thus, by a kind of paradox, Christianity tended to preserve, almost against its will, ways of thinking that had come into existence with the Greeks and thus inadvertently helped to carry the Hellenic tradition of rationality over into western thought. In this respect, as in its institutionalization, Christianity made a unique contribution to the development of the western tradition. Other great religions approached this sophisticated level of theological speculation for longer or shorter periods of time, but none continued the practice so consistently over so many centuries. If this strange circumstance had not occurred, it is hard to imagine how the later western intellectual tradition could have come into being.

We must also remember that as Christianity inadvertently, indeed almost accidently, kept alive the Greek ways of rational thinking, it more consciously preserved the outlook of another ancient people. Christianity extended forward in time certain of the uniquely significant assumptions about God, man, and history first enunciated by the prophets of Israel. History was not purposeless in the Christian view. It moved toward a rendezvous at the end of time. No event, therefore, was ever meaningless or random. It was always a part of God's divine plan for the world. Moreover, men knew how they were expected to participate in this plan. They were expected to obey the ethical injunctions of God. In this way the western tradition was infused and informed by a set of moral assumptions, which, though often imperfectly realized, later guided much of western social and political development.

The assumptions that history is purposeful and that it must eventuate in a period of a thousand years of perfect bliss before the final divine judgment had important recurring effects within the Christian community over the centuries. It tended, for one, to perpetuate an expectation among believers that the last days were not far off and that men, as a result, must prepare themselves in special ways for the final event (apocalypse). Furthermore, this assumption was reinforced by the book of the New Testament known as Revelation (whose authorship is ascribed to the apostle John), which seemed to promise a speedy return of Christ to this world in preparation for a final rendezvous at the end of history. Thus Christianity, like Judaism, tended to foster hopes of Messianic deliverance from the evils of this world at some future time, "when God shall wipe away all tears from their eyes; and there shall be no more death, neither sorrow, nor crying, nor shall there be any more pain; for the former things are passed away." As a

B. GERMANIC INFLUENCES: THE RISE OF FEUDALISM

1. GERMANIC INVASIONS

a. Vandals, 406–548. Entered Gaul, 406; crossed into Spain (409) and Africa (429), where they established a kingdom that lasted until 534, when it was finally conquered by Emperor Justinian.

b. Ostrogoths (East Goths). Invasion of Italy by Theodoric the Ostrogoth, 488; establishment of Ostrogothic kingdom of Italy, 493–535. Reconquest of Italy by Justinian, 535–554

c. Visigoths (West Goths). Invaded Spain, 415. Visigothic kingdom of Spain established, 466–711. Conversion of Visigoths to Latin Christianity, 587. Beginning of Islamic conquest of Spain (battle of Guadalete), 711.

d. Lombards. Invaded Italy, 568; conquered northern and central areas, 568–605. Converted to Latin Christianity, ca. 650. Lombard kingdom absorbed into the Frankish empire of Charlemagne, 774.

e. Franks. Penetrated into Gaul at the end of the fourth century. Consolidation of the Frankish kingdom under Clovis, 481–511. Merovingian king-

consequence of the prevalence of this expectation, from time to time in the history of Christianity there appeared significant groups of people who saw in the failure of the Christian Church as an institution or in the shortcomings of their fellow Christians reasons for believing that the prophecies about the last days were soon to be fulfilled. Quite frequently this concern with the malfunction of the church gave rise to substantial heretical movements, the most famous of which resulted in the Protestant Reformation of the sixteenth century.

There is a double importance in this phenomenon of Messianic expectation. First, the recurring discontent with the ruling authority of the church and with official morality among Christians meant that Christianity was continually in danger of serious division of the kind that occurred in 1054 when the Eastern Orthodox church divided from the Roman church and in 1517 with the Lutheran revolt. Second, the continual renewal of expectations that the last days were at hand accustomed men to the notion that some great transformation in human circumstances would some day occur and alter the world of men completely. The millennial vision (after the word "millennium," meaning the thousand years of peace and holiness before the last judgment) was one of the reasons for the rise of the Great Revolutionary Idea, which would later have such effect on world history (*see* pp. 11–12).

B. GERMANIC INFLUENCES: THE RISE OF FEUDALISM

With the disappearance of Rome's centralized authority in the fifth century and the emergence of the Germanic successor kingdoms, the society of the old western Roman provinces began to change. In part this transformation was the result of a decline in city life, outside Italy in particular, and the disappearance of the forms of economic organization that had made possible the existence of the highly centralized, bureaucratic Roman state. Necessity thus drove the inhabitants of the empire to localize their government and other institutions in order to secure themselves against attack and to become economically self-sufficient. The customary unit of such organization was the great estate (manor), whose owner became the patron of a large number of dependents, from whom he received labor in return for protection and food.

As the Germanic tribes moved into the empire, this system was slowly fused with the Germanic tribal custom by which the members of a tribal war band bound themselves in an oath of loyalty to their chief. From these two distinct Roman and German sources there evolved the system of social organization usually described as feudalism. Under feudalism the basic economic and political unit was the

dom of the Franks taken over by the descendants of Charles Martel
(481–754). Pepin the Short crowned king of the Franks, 754. Charlemagne
(Charles the Great) ruled as king of the Franks, 768–814, and as Roman
emperor of the West, 800–814.

f. Anglo-Saxons. Roman legions withdrawn from Britain, 407–422.
Angles, Saxons, and Jutes invaded England from the European continent,
ca. 450–615. Anglo-Saxon heptarchy (seven small kingdoms) united under
Alfred the Great (871–899), king of Wessex, and his two sons, Edward
(899–924) and Athelstane (924–939).

2. MANORIALISM

The manor or estate was the economic and social unit of medieval life. Like
a modern farm, it varied in size from a few to many thousands of acres. It
was the manor, worked by serfs or tenants of its lord or holder, that provided subsistence for feudal society. Most of those who worked the manor
were serfs or "unfree" men (they were not slaves in the sense that their
bodies were owned by a master, since they could not be removed from the
manor) bound to the manor and obligated to furnish uncompensated
labor on the lord's lands as well as a portion of their own crops. The lord
himself was usually not the outright owner of his manor in the modern
sense but held it under the authority of someone else for whom he was
obligated to do certain services. For the lord and those like him higher
up the feudal social ladder, this relationship, was not servile like that between the serf and the lord of the manor; rather it was honorable under
terms of the feudal contract (see below).

3. FEUDALISM AND THE FEUDAL CONTRACT

Feudalism was a set of contractual arrangements under which most of
feudal society was governed. As a system of government, it was neither
inherently evil nor inferior to other systems. In a sense, it was simply a
necessary means of operating an agricultural society that had no strong centralized government and had to protect itself against invasion and preserve
the stability of its social relations and institutions. The binding element of
feudal society, therefore, was the feudal contract between lords and vassals,
who made up the ruling nonservile classes of that society (serfs or unfree
men were not a part of the feudal contract). In this contract the vassal
(lesser lord) in return for his land formally acknowledged the suzerain
(higher lord) as his overlord and did homage. Thus the suzerain was assured
that the vassal would undertake to furnish his feudal superior certain
services, usually of a military nature, and the vassal was assured of protection in return. In order for the system to work, the vassal had to have land

manorial estate, which provided society, with subsistence and military power. Social relationships between lord and vassal were governed by the feudal contract, which laid down their reciprocal obligations. In modern times it has been customary to regard feudalism as a repressive and dangerously decentralizing form of social and political organization. It should be remembered, however, that in spite of its shortcomings in modern eyes, it was the only means of providing security and social stability over fairly broad areas in societies that were predominantly agricultural.

The feudal-manorial system in its fully developed form was not reached until later in the Middle Ages. In the period between the fifth and seventh centuries it had not yet come into being in the strictest sense, for this was the time when the Germanic invaders of empire were only beginning to establish themselves in regions that would later become the feudal kingdoms of the High Middle Ages and, at a more remote date, the national monarchies of early modern Europe. To a large extent, in fact, it may be said that historical chance determined these later developments, for the original regions where these Germanic tribes settled were where they happened to find themselves by luck or conquest at a particular moment in time.

Who were the Germans? Their origins are obscure, but from what we can determine from archeological evidence they appear to have been one of several waves of invaders who began to move outward from Scandinavia sometime about 1000 B.C. If the evidence is correct it would thus appear that they were related ethnically to the later Vikings (see pp. 80–83). Historians have long puzzled over the reasons why this movement, known commonly by the German word *Völkerwänderungen* (wanderings of the peoples), should have occurred. At present we have no clear and positive explanation. These movements may have taken place out of a desire for plunder, because of food shortages, pressure of other peoples, or perhaps simply because the Germanic tribes were driven by the characteristic restlessness of all nomadic peoples. In any event, the most important of these Germanic tribes (Goths, Vandals, Burgundians, and Alemanni) apparently had reached the Rhine and the Danube basin sometime about 100 B.C. They might well have conquered Gaul (France) had not Roman military power thrust them back to the Rhine frontier where large numbers of them settled permanently. In the fourth and fifth centuries, however, when the imperial frontier collapsed, certain German tribes —Vandals, Visigoths, Franks—penetrated territories lying west of the Rhine. At about the same time the Germanic Angles and Saxons began the conquest of the Roman province of Britain.

Germanic Influences: The Rise of Feudalism 75

for his own subsistence and the subsistence of those dependent upon him and to provide the services for which he was obligated to the suzerain. Thus it was that landholding and the obligations attached to it were absolutely essential to the existence of feudalism and determined a man's social as well as his economic position in society.

C. THE EARLY DIVISION OF CHRISTENDOM AND THE BYZANTINE EAST

Death of Emperor Justinian (565) ended hopes of reuniting the eastern and and western halves of the Roman Empire; the Eastern or Byzantine Empire remained the sole heir to Rome's power. With the passage of time, however, it ceased to be Roman and became almost completely Greek in language and culture.

Loss of Italian possessions to the Lombards, 568–571. Beginning of Islamic conquest of the Eastern Empire, 635–655. Constantinople besieged by Moslems, 673–678 and 717–718. Missionary activities of saints Cyril and Methodius paved the way for conversion of the Slavic peoples to Orthodox Christianity, 863–865. Prince Vladimir of Russia converted, 989. Final religious schism between Rome and Constantinople, 1054.

Victory of the Seljuk Turks over the Byzantines at Manzikert (1071) marked the beginning of Byzantine decline. Conquest and sack of Constantinople by western Crusaders (Fourth Crusade), 1204. Latin kingdom of Constantinople established, 1204–1261. Reconquest of Constantinople by Emperor Michael VIII, 1261. Rise of the Ottoman Turks in Asia Minor, 1326. Siege and capture of Constantinople by the Ottoman Turks resulting in end of the Eastern Empire, 1453.

The Problem of the Great Schism between East and West: Though theological differences and missionary rivalries were the obvious reasons for the division between the Greek Orthodox and the Latin Churches in 1054, there are certain other things about the relations between the two that need to be known in order to understand their attitudes toward one another

What we know of these early Germans comes to us from thin and scattered sources. Only one written work descriptive of them, the *Germania* composed by the Roman historian Tacitus in A.D. 98, has survived. Otherwise we are forced to rely upon bits of surviving folk literature, compilations of Germanic laws, and archaeology. On these bases an earlier generation of historians built up an idealized and romanticized picture of these tribesmen as brave, strong lovers of freedom who gave a distinctive cast to later European legal and political traditions. This is an exaggeration. Nevertheless, some few of their customs did have later influences. Perhaps more important, however, though their coming in great numbers contributed to the final breakdown of Roman imperial government, they were converted to Latin Christianity over a period of time. In this way, they helped to create the later medieval European community of Christendom and thus contributed to the making of Europe.

C. THE EARLY DIVISION OF CHRISTENDOM AND THE BYZANTINE EAST

So long as the Roman Empire in the West existed and for some centuries thereafter, the Christian world, though periodically torn by controversy, maintained a nominal unity under the headship of the bishops of Rome (the popes), who, from their central position at the heart of the empire, were able to assert and maintain claims to supremacy over the whole Christian church. With the establishment in the East of a new capital, Constantinople (Byzantium), in the early fourth century, the eastern and western halves of the empire gradually became separate units of ecclesiastical as well as political administration. When the western half of the empire fell, the eastern half continued in existence and insisted, with some justice, that it was the true inheritor of Rome's power. Under Emperor Justinian (527–565) the Eastern Empire strove to restore Roman unity by conquering the western provinces. When this effort failed, the Eastern Roman empire fell back upon its own resources and took on the cultural characteristics and language of its Greek surroundings. It was profoundly Christian, and its church, the spiritual predecessor of the modern Eastern Orthodox churches, remained in communion with Rome and recognized, at least nominally, the supremacy of the Pope.

In spite of their common Christian heritage, the Byzantine Empire and the Roman West were increasingly isolated from one another during the early Middle Ages. The Eastern Empire was continually involved in a struggle to preserve the old eastern Roman heritage from

over the centuries. While the dispute that led to their division in 1054 was a result of theological disagreement over the use of images in churches, it must also be remembered that the two churches were growing further apart because of cultural and ethnic differences and that the Byzantine church had to consider political as well as religious divergences among the various peoples who inhabited the Eastern Empire. In this latter respect, the Eastern church was never as free as the Western Latin church. It was, after all, a department of the state, in a sense, as the Western church was not; therefore, it could not be so firm about matters of religious orthodoxy as the Latin church was. Thus, when Rome commanded the Byzantine church to deal summarily with religious dissenters, the Eastern church could not always do so for political reasons. Nevertheless, over the centuries—and, indeed, down to our own time—the two churches have remained very close to one another so far as basic theological assumptions, liturgical forms, and ecclesiastical practices are concerned.

D. THE SIEGE OF EUROPE: MOSLEM, VIKING, AND MAGYAR

1. THE RISE OF ISLAM

a. Life of Muhammad, 570–638. Born at Mecca, 570. Flight (hegira) from Mecca to Medina, 622, altered the character of the new Islamic sect and gave it an opportunity for broader appeal. Compilation of the Koran (the sacred book of Islam), 622–632, revealed the strong ethical bases of Islam and its spiritual strength, which attracted the Arab tribes. Organization of the commonwealth of Islam at Medina, 622–630. At Muhammad's death, 632, Islam had already displayed the expansionist tendencies that marked its later growth.

b. Expansion of Islam, 632–1491. Conquest of Syria, 634–641; Persia, 635–641; Egypt, 639–644; North Africa, 643–711; Spain, 711–715. Invasion of southern France and defeat at Tours by Charles Martel, 732. Breakup of the first great Islamic Empire began, ca. 750. Seljuk Turks attacked and took Babylon, 1055. Christian crusaders from the West established the kingdom of Jerusalem, 1099–1187. Christian reconquest of Spain, 1072–1491. Rise of the Ottoman Turks (fourteenth century) led finally to their domination of the Moslem world by the mid-fifteenth century.

successive waves of invaders. Though it faced grave difficulties this Greek empire made skillful use of its military resources and managed to keep its independence and make Constantinople the center of a brilliant civilization for nearly a thousand years. Confident that the Eastern Empire was the true Rome and that its civilization was superior to that of the Germanized West (as it was), the Greek church grew increasingly restive at the claims of the Roman popes to speak for the whole Christian church. Theological controversy, further aggravated by missionary rivalry (the Greek church had been successful in carrying its form of Christianity to the Slavic peoples of eastern and northern Europe), finally led in 1054 to a schism that was to divide the Latin and Greek churches thereafter.

Apart from the problem of religion, the existence of the Eastern Empire was of profound importance to the West in other ways. For centuries Constantinople was a bulwark against invaders who might otherwise have made their way deep into the heart of western Europe. At the same time, during periods of peace, it was a major exchange point for trade between the West and the Asiatic hinterland.

D. THE SIEGE OF EUROPE: MOSLEM, VIKING, AND MAGYAR

Though the formation of Europe as we know it in modern times was largely accomplished by the eleventh century, the process was continually interrupted and, on occasion, even checked by the threat of outside invasion. If there was any period of Europe's formative stage when Western civilization's future development seemed to be seriously threatened, it was from the eighth through the early eleventh centuries, when a succession of invaders kept the various regions in constant turmoil by continuous attacks and threats of conquest. Looking backward, we can see that the threats from all sources—Moslems, Vikings, and Magyars (Hungarians)—were not so serious as they seemed to contemporaries or to a later generation of scholars who saw in each of these groups a threat to the very possibility of western development. Even by the end of the eighth century the absorptive powers of Christendom were such that no conqueror unless he had come in overwhelming numbers could have altered the course of European history permanently. Nevertheless, the constant threat and endless harassment of raids and full-scale invasions certainly impeded developments that might have moved more quickly had Europe been free of external threats and alarms during the period in question. In

c. The Religious Teachings of Islam. The emergence of Islam as a major religion during the early Middle Ages was of enormous importance in the development of medieval Europe. Not only did many of the writings of the ancient world pass through the hands of Moslem scholars before being transmitted to the Latin West, but Islam by its very existence challenged the religious community of Christendom in a number of stimulating ways.

The important religious fact about Islam from its very beginning was its direct and simple appeal to the ethical understanding of the peoples to whom it was preached. Muhammad was not a sophisticated scholar or subtle thinker, and therein lay much of the success of the religion he founded. The teaching of Islam was unambiguous and easily comprehended. Allah, the Supreme Being of Islam, is a single all-powerful, all-knowing God in the great monotheistic tradition of Judaism and Christianity. Unlike Christianity, however, Islam did not have to develop a complex theology to explain the nature of a divine Trinity or why it was that God should have chosen to appear on earth in human form in order to suffer on the cross. Muhammad was not "a partaker of divinity." He was only the last and greatest of the prophets, "the seal of the prophets." Abraham and Christ, according to the Koran, were earlier prophets who simply prepared the way for the coming of Muhammad.

Furthermore, the ethical injunctions laid down in the Koran are stern and demandingly puritanical. The word "Islam" means "submission to the will of Allah." Allah rewards those who obey his commands and punishes those who do not. Faithful Moslems are expected to pray regularly and to visit the holy places at Mecca at least once in their lives. They are also expected to avoid drinking and gambling, deal with their fellow men in justice and mercy, practice charity, and adhere to a rigorous code of sexual morality (though the Moslem who can afford it is permitted to have four wives). And, finally, the Moslem is expected to defend the true faith with his very life, if necessary—a requirement that has made Islam one of the most militant of all religions. The really great mass appeal of Islam lies in the essential clarity of its ethical demands: there are no doubts as to whether the good man may perish or the evil prosper; the commands of Allah, if obeyed, will give the righteous their due reward without doubt or question.

2. VIKING AND MAGYAR (HUNGARIAN) INVASIONS, 787–1091

First invasion of England by the Danes, 787; continued in force, 856–875. Siege of Paris by Norsemen, 886. Magyars (Hungarians) invaded central Europe and northern Italy, ca. 900; defeated at Lechfeld by Emperor Otto I, 955. Founding of the duchy of Normandy by Rollo the Norseman, 911. Danish kings ruled England, 1013–1041. Norman conquest of southern Italy,

any event, the emergence of strong feudal monarchies by the end of the eleventh century put an end to the social chaos attendant upon the constant threat of invasion from outside Christendom.

1. THE RISE OF ISLAM

Of all the threats of invasion and conquest the most dangerous were presented by the followers of Islam (the name that all Moslems give to their religion); for though the Viking raids were disastrous, the Norsemen were ultimately Christianized and brought into the community of Europe, but the Moslems never were so assimilated. The Moslems were followers of the desert prophet Muhammad (570–632), who in the seventh century had aroused the zeal of the nomad peoples of Arabia by presenting them with a new religious revelation. Inspired by the new faith to embark upon a series of conquests, the followers of Islam, with their superior military skills and high level of civilization, ultimately menaced the security of early medieval Europe.

Beginning in the seventh century, the Moslems spread rapidly outward from the Arabian peninsula and by the opening of the eighth century had brought under their control large parts of the Near and Middle East, all of North Africa, and Spain. In the West this expansion was finally checked by the Germanic (Frankish) inhabitants of France at the battle of Tours in 732. In the East, however, though the leadership of Islam later passed from the Arabs to the Seljuk Turks and later still to the Ottoman Turks, a relentless, centuries-long pressure against Constantinople finally led to that city's capture in 1453 and the Islamic conquest of large areas in southeastern Europe.

In spite of the inveterate hostility between Christian and Moslem, it was from the great Islamic centers of learning, particularly in Spain, that much knowledge of ancient civilization lost to the West since Rome's fall came to be known in medieval Europe. Moslem scholars translated and preserved the works of Aristotle, which were later introduced into thirteenth-century Europe with enormous intellectual impact. Moreover, the techniques and skills of Arab traders, the mathematics of Arab savants, and the scientific devices of Arab technology contributed much to the medieval West.

2. VIKING AND MAGYAR (HUNGARIAN) INVASIONS, 787–1091

The causes of the great Viking invasions of Europe are still something of a mystery. A desire for loot and plunder is not alone sufficient to explain why these bands of freebooters irrupted into Europe with such force and frequency during the early Middle Ages. Their raids came in

1042–1068. Invasion and conquest of England by William of Normandy (battle of Hastings), 1066. Last Viking invasion of England, 1076. Normans conquered Sicily, 1072–1091, and established kingdom of Sicily, 1091–1266.

waves of varying intensity and frequently were separated by long periods of quiescence. Apparently a combination of causes—hope of gain, the political disunity of ancient Scandinavia, and population pressures in their homelands—drove them forth to plunder the coasts of Europe for more than 400 years. Once they had been converted to Christianity, however, they rapidly assimilated to the customs and traditions of Western Christendom. Rapacious in their desire for plunder and irrational in the heat of battle, nonetheless they were people of intelligence and energy who ruled the lands they conquered with skill. By the eleventh century the Vikings had established a group of feudal states whose stability and administrative efficiency made them unique in medieval Europe. In northern France they founded the duchy of Normandy, whose power rivaled that of French kings; in Italy they founded the kingdom of Sicily. Their greatest success, however, came with the Norman conquest of England in 1066, as a result of which they were able to create the strongest and most highly centralized of feudal monarchies. In the twelfth and thirteenth centuries their remote colony of Iceland on the farthest edge of the medieval world was to develop a native literature unequaled for its vigor and brilliance anywhere in Europe.

The Magyars (Hungarians) were a Turco-Mongol people who invaded Europe along the route out of Asia that had been followed by countless nomadic invaders since prehistoric times. For several decades from the late ninth century onward these mounted warriors threatened the peace and security of central Europe and northern Italy. Their depredations received a severe check at the battle of Riade (933), where they were defeated by the Saxon emperor Henry I the Fowler (919–936); they were finally stopped completely and diverted to a settled life by their defeat at the hands of Emperor Otto I (936–973) at Lechfeld (955). From that time forward the Hungarians became a permanent ethnic community in the region of central Europe that bears their name to this day.

With the end of these external threats of invasion and the growing strength of the feudal monarchies, medieval Europe entered upon a long process of internal consolidation. That is not to say, of course, that serious invasion attempts from outside Europe ceased altogether. The thirteenth century witnessed the Mongol invasion that in 1241 destroyed German, Polish, and Hungarian armies and left Europe defenseless. Europe was saved only by a dynastic crisis in the Mongol empire, which forced the Mongol invaders to withdraw. Later, the Ottoman Turks would conquer much of southeastern Europe and threaten to take Vienna twice—in 1529 and 1683; but these were very

E. RECONSOLIDATION OF THE WEST: REVIVAL OF THE IMPERIAL IDEA

1. CHARLEMAGNE'S EMPIRE, 768–814

Accession of Charlemagne to Frankish throne, 768. Defeated Lombards in Italy and assumed title of king, 773–774. Conquered the Saxons, 785; Bavarians, 787–788; and Avars, 795–796. Pope Leo III crowned Charlemagne emperor of the West at Rome, 800. Death of Charlemagne, 814.

2. SUCCESSORS OF CHARLEMAGNE, 814–987

Reign of Louis the Pious, 814–840. Treaty of Verdun, 843, divided empire among three heirs and thus separated the historical areas of modern France and Germany. Henry the Fowler became king of Germany, 919–936. Otto the Great of Germany crowned emperor at Rome, 962; beginning of the Germanization of the Holy Roman Empire. Hugh Capet crowned king of France, 987.

3. THE CAROLINGIAN RENAISSANCE

Charlemagne reestablished the palace school for the improvement of ecclesiastical learning under the direction of Alcuin of York, 782–796. He also founded libraries for the preservation of Latin manuscripts and restored classical learning through the promotion of scholarship. The important thing about Carolingian society, however, apart from its purely intellectual achievements, was that Charlemagne tried to apply intelligence and rationalized practices to the affairs of government. Unfortunately, neither the resources nor the number of educated persons was sufficient to guarantee the permanence of Carolingian administrative effectiveness.

different ventures from the constant harassment of the Magyar, Moslem, and Viking raids. The important point is that by the eleventh century Christendom had won breathing space for its own internal development; henceforth the only dangers to its stability and future development were internal rather than external.

E. RECONSOLIDATION OF THE WEST: REVIVAL OF THE IMPERIAL IDEA

By the end of the eighth century at least one of the Germanic successor states, the kingdom of the Franks (which comprised almost all of modern France and part of modern Germany), seemed capable of restoring the lost unity of the Western Empire. The hope of such a restoration had been kept alive by the papacy, and that hope seemed to become a reality with the rise to power of the strong Frankish king Charlemagne (768–814). Under him the kingdom of the Franks had become a great military power with a remarkably efficient feudal government. Unfortunately for papal desires, these characteristics alone were not sufficient to make Charlemagne's realm into a new Roman Empire. No feudal society could successfully reproduce the centralized bureaucracy or maintain the permanent tax-supported military organization of the earlier empire. Without these, reviving Rome's universal dominion was impossible. Nonetheless, the effort was made by Pope Leo III who, on Christmas Day in the year 800, crowned Charlemagne Emperor of the West. In the end, this coronation proved to be a futile gesture; for, despite his great unifying achievement and his success in reintroducing the lost cultural traditions of antiquity to the northern European peoples (Carolingian Renaissance), Charlemagne's empire scarcely outlasted his own lifetime. After his death it was divided among his descendants, and the division was confirmed permanently by the Treaty of Verdun in 843.

Undeterred by this initial failure, later popes attempted once again to revive the empire; in the tenth century they helped create the Holy Roman Empire by crowning the German prince Otto the Great as emperor. By that time, however, it was already too late. The various feudal kingdoms of the West were too strong and too firmly entrenched to surrender their sovereignty to any imperial overlord, even one backed by the authority of the papacy.

chapter six

EVENTS AND DEFINITIONS

A. THE MEDIEVAL PAPACY AND THE IDEA OF UNIVERSALITY

Foundation of the monastery of Cluny, 910; spread of its influence, 910–950. The monk Hildebrand (later Pope Gregory VII) led the reform movement in the church, 1054–1085. As pope he forced Emperor Henry IV to submit to papal authority by a public act of penance at Canossa, 1077.

The High
Middle Ages

THE ESSENTIAL MOVEMENT

The period of the High Middle Ages (twelfth through fourteenth centuries) saw the culmination of what is now recognized as a great civilization. In those three centuries many isolated and scattered strands of historical development came together to form a complex cultural unity, which, while it accepted the goals and aspirations of Christian belief, was nonetheless freer in expression and more diverse in its interests than former historians were wont to think. This civilization contributed far more to the development of some of the later institutions and traditions of the modern world than was previously thought. Far from having been a time of repression and stagnation, this era of history was in fact a period of great achievement and originality.

A. THE MEDIEVAL PAPACY AND THE IDEA OF UNIVERSALITY

The High Middle Ages marked the peak of papal power and authority, culminating in the pontificate of Innocent III (1198–1216). This development was the result of a number of revolutionary changes that made the medieval church an effective international administrative system run by an intellectual elite of men whose training and abilities were far

Gregorian reform movement. This movement was not simply an extension of the earlier Cluniac reform movement mentioned in Section A (Essential Movement). It was in many ways a totally new movement, which came into being as the original reforming impulses of the older Cluniac movement died away. Its three other great leaders (apart from Pope Gregory VII, 1073–1085) were Paschal II (1099–1118) and two cardinals, Peter Damiani (d. 1072) and Humbert of Silva Candida (d. 1061). These four men not only were responsible for the rejuvenation of the life of the church and the exaltation of papal authority but also stimulated an intense piety that reached out to every corner of Christendom. This new piety made it possible for the papacy of the twelfth and thirteenth centuries to direct and guide the affairs of medieval Europe as no other single institution has ever done in history. Men came to believe in the truth of Christian revelation and the church's teachings as never before or since. Some scholars have even argued that this change was so radical as to constitute a great revolution in men's ways of thought and action. Though this conclusion has been questioned by other historians, it is true that the church's authority did depend upon the important fact that large numbers of human beings were willing to accept its teachings unquestioningly. Furthermore, this new and intense piety prepared the way for the founding of the two greatest of medieval mendicant (begging) monastic orders: the Franciscans founded by Saint Francis of Assisi (1182–1226) and the Dominicans founded by Saint Dominic (1170–1221). From the latter order came Thomas Aquinas (1225–1274), the greatest of medieval scholastic philosophers.

Proclamation of the first crusade by Pope Urban II, 1095.

Compromise over lay investiture in England and France, 1107. Concordat of Worms, 1122, settled differences between pope and Holy Roman Emperor over lay investiture in German lands.

Innocent III (1198–1216) asserted the supremacy of the papacy over all Christendom: forced John of England to acknowledge the pope as feudal overlord, 1213; suppressed Albigensian heresy in the south of France by formal crusade, 1208–1213. Under Pope Innocent the medieval church reached its highest peak of administrative effectiveness. Innocent's reforms and changes were summed up in the decrees of the Fourth Lateran Council (1215). It was this council that first clearly defined the seven sacraments as baptism, holy eucharist, confession (penance), confirmation, marriage, ordination, and extreme unction. Boniface VIII (1294–1303) became the last of the all-powerful popes, as the "Babylonian captivity" (1305–1376) saw the papacy transferred to Avignon in the south of France where popes fell under the influence of French kings.

The Great Schism (1378–1417) marked the division of the church between two rival popes. John Wyclif initiated the Lollard movement in

greater than those of the rest of society. Through the patient work of these men over many generations, the church was largely freed of its dependence upon nobles and kings, and the papal office was made the focus of an administrative authority that reached into every corner of Latin Christendom.

The revolution that made these changes possible began in the tenth century with the founding of the Cluniac order of monks (named for the abbey of Cluny in southern France). By stressing the importance of monastic discipline in their personal lives and of canon (church) law in the conduct of ecclesiastical business, the monks of Cluny initiated a vast reform movement in the church during the tenth and eleventh centuries. As a result, many serious ecclesiastical abuses were corrected and, more important, the right to choose the popes passed into the control of an elective body (the college of cardinals) and out of the hands of the Holy Roman emperors who had previously nominated the pontiffs. Once the churchmen had freed their own highest office of lay control, they pushed other reforms with such vigor that the quality of the clergy steadily improved and the standards of religious teaching rose throughout medieval Europe. The victory was not easily won, however. The Holy Roman emperors and most other secular rulers were opposed to an independent clergy that might challenge their own authority. Furthermore, they were anxious to retain the right of nomination to high ecclesiastical office within their own territories since by reason of their offices the archbishops, bishops, and abbots were usually also feudal landholders or state officials with so much secular authority that no king could safely allow the church to have the sole power of choosing them. While the papacy gained its own independence, therefore, it had to struggle throughout the Middle Ages for the right to nominate other high ecclesiastical officeholders. In this conflict over lay investiture the church's weapons were excommunication (the power to deny an individual the sacraments—i.e., baptism, communion, confirmation, etc.) and interdict (the power to cut off an entire country from the ministrations of religion in order to force its rulers to submit). These potent weapons were sufficient, in an age when men accepted the church's spiritual authority without question, to make the popes nominal overlords of all Christendom. The assumption that justified this great authority was based upon an ancient claim long accepted by the supporters of papal supremacy but seldom put into practice before the eleventh century. This was the claim that the popes, as a consequence of the power originally conferred by Christ upon St. Peter, the first pontiff, were responsible as Christ's vicars for the spiritual welfare of all mankind, while secular rulers were responsi-

England by challenging the church's theology, 1380. Wyclifite influence gave rise to the Hussite heresy (named for John Hus) in Bohemia, ca. 1400. Council of Constance ended the Great Schism and restored the unity of the papacy, 1414–1418.

B. THE RISE OF THE FEUDAL MONARCHIES

1. ENGLAND, 1066–1485

Conquest of England by William Duke of Normandy in 1066 introduced the continental system of feudalism and established a tradition of strong and effective kingship. Beginning with William the Conqueror (1066–1087) and continuing through the reigns of three strong kings—Henry I (1100–1135), Henry II (1154–1189), and Edward I (1272–1307)—England developed the most effectively centralized feudal state in Europe. At the same time English kings embarked upon a policy of expansion that saw a large part of the British Isles brought under their rule and made them at various times until the middle of the fifteenth century masters of great territorial holdings in France.

a. Development of the English State. *Domesday Book* (1086) surveyed the whole of England and gave to English kings a body of statistical information not available to other feudal monarchs. Organization of the Exchequer in the reign of Henry I (1100–1135) facilitated the relatively efficient

ble only for the welfare of their own subjects—and only in this world. As a natural conclusion of this theory, it was believed by papal supporters that the power of the popes was universal and thus transcended the authority of temporal monarchs. The pope, then, was accountable for the "cure of souls"; and, since this responsibility was a far greater one than that of any king, conflicts between the spiritual and temporal powers had to be resolved in favor of the former. On the basis of this claim, Pope Innocent III, in the thirteenth century, was able to assert not only a spiritual but also a feudal lordship over all the Latin West.

The last strong pope of the High Middle Ages, Boniface VIII (1294–1303), was the author of the most extreme assertions of papal power ever made. His position was set forth in two famous documents, *Clericis Laicos* (1296) and *Unam Sanctam* (1302). In the first he prohibited the taxing of the clergy by the kings of England and France without express papal permission. In the second he put forward a claim to be universal monarch of all Christendom by stating that "for every human creature to be subject to the Roman pontiff is absolutely necessary for salvation." At the very time these words were published, the papacy was being challenged most seriously by the French king, Philip the Fair (1285–1314), whose representative actually captured the pope and kept him prisoner for a brief time. The act was more than symbolic, for it marked the beginning of the long decline of the medieval papacy.

B. THE RISE OF THE FEUDAL MONARCHIES

Despite the papacy's great success, medieval kings contrived to hold their own in the struggle and even to expand their powers. To do so they had to accomplish two things: first, they had to destroy the localized authority of great feudal nobles whose power often threatened their own; and, second, they had to create a centralized government bureaucracy that would enable them to rule without having to depend upon the churchmen or the great feudal lords for the carrying on of the routine business of state. They moved toward these goals not with any carefully thought-out long-range plan but by day-to-day effort. Sometimes the royal power was checked and the process of expansion slowed or even reversed, but over the centuries the royal power grew steadily until the highly centralized, absolute monarchies of the early modern period had come into being.

During all this time European kings had to perform a skillful political juggling act. On the one hand they had to make use of the church and churchmen to strengthen royal government and weaken

collection of the king's revenues. Permanent court of professional judges organized (1178), out of which evolved the later courts of common law (King's Bench, Exchequer, and Common Pleas). English barons forced John (1199–1216) to sign the Great Charter (Magna Carta; 1215) and thus to recognize the validity of the feudal contract; limited the power of the king. Simon de Montfort, head of a faction of rebellious barons, summoned a parliament, 1265. Edward I called first "model" parliament in 1295. Parliament developed and became a permanent English institution during the fourteenth and fifteenth centuries. Social unrest of the Hundred Years War led to Peasants' Revolt, 1381. Period of anarchy in the mid-fourteenth century culminated in Wars of the Roses, civil strife between two rival factions for control of the English throne, 1455–1485. Henry VII defeated Richard III at battle of Bosworth (1485) to end civil wars and restore order.

b. Expansion of England, 1066–1485.   First English invasion of Ireland, 1169. Loss of the duchy of Normandy to France, 1204. Conquest of Wales, 1276–1284. Edward I attempted to conquer Scotland, 1292–1307; Scots defeated his son, Edward II, at Bannockburn, 1314. Independence of Scotland recognized at Treaty of Northampton, 1328. Outbreak of the Hundred Years' War (1337–1453) between England and France saw England at first victorious under Edward III (1327–1377) and later under Henry V (1413–1422); England finally forced to relinquish all its French possessions but Calais.

2.   FRANCE, 987–1483

The great problems of the medieval French monarchy were to curb the power of a strong feudal nobility and, in the later Middle Ages, to win back lands that had been lost to England and the dukes of Burgundy. The first problem was doubly difficult for the French kings, because they had not conquered France as William the Conqueror had England, but were in fact only the greatest of feudal landholders—and sometimes not even that. What they had to do gradually over many generations was conquer their own nobles and make them obey royal law. Under a series of strong kings, whose good fortune it was to remain unbroken in the male line between 987 and 1328, the French monarchy steadily extended its power outward from the environs of Paris by marriage and conquest. The most important of these kings were Hugh Capet (the founder of the Capetian line), 987–996; Philip II (Augustus), 1180–1223, who won back the duchy of Normandy from England in 1204; Louis IX (St. Louis, the crusading king), 1226–1270; and Philip IV (the Fair), 1285–1314.

a.   The Hundred Years' War, 1337–1453.   The Hundred Years' War, a long and disastrous interlude in the history of both France and England, began

the feudal nobility. To do so, they borrowed from the church the administrative techniques and experience that only the church possessed. On the other hand, they had to be careful not to make the church itself so strong that it would become, in the end, as dangerous to their authority as the feudal nobles. This problem was further intensified by the difficulty of financing the kind of government sought by the kings through the methods available in a feudal society. Royal revenues took the form not of regularly stipulated payments from all their subjects for the support of the state but of feudal dues or aids, which were granted the king by his vassals on some extraordinary occasion when the king's own income was insufficient. The regular income that went to pay for the king's personal needs and to support the developing bureaucracy of the royal household had to come from the rents on his own personal estates (demesne lands). From the twelfth century onward one of the major tasks of the feudal monarch was thus to preserve and increase his personal lands and, since the revenues from these were not sufficient to meet all his needs, to convert the irregular feudal dues into a regular form of revenue. In attempting to do these things, however, medieval kings further strained their relations with the church on one side and the feudal nobles on the other.

The conflict with the church was intensified because the thirteenth century had seen the consummation of that internal administrative revolution in ecclesiastical government begun about 300 years before. The great autonomous, international bureaucracy of the church had need not only of great financial resources but also of intellectually trained manpower. Since both were limited and both were demanded by church and state alike, the competition between popes and kings for these inadequate resources was intense. Both simultaneously brought pressures to bear on feudal society and each, in so doing, sought to limit the other's right to make use of lands and revenues. In the desperate search for new revenues, medieval kings fell back upon a device that in time, would lead to even greater conflicts between themselves and their subjects. It was during this period that feudal representative assemblies—the English Parliament, French Estates General, German Diet—came into existence. Though the concept of representative government had long been known in the church and had been carried over into secular government in many localized areas of Europe, medieval monarchs in the thirteenth and fourteenth centuries began to make greater use of it to serve their own financial and administrative needs. Monarchs found it to their advantage to consult with the representatives of all the important feudal classes or estates in order to secure their cooperation in getting money for the royal treasury. The latter,

with English successes at Crécy (1346) and Poitiers (1356) that led to the conquest of extensive French territories. The war started for three causes: (1) the ambitions of Edward III of England (1327–1377); (2) the lack of a male heir to the French monarchy at the death of the last Capetian king in 1328, which opened the door to claims by Edward III, whose mother was a French princess; and (3) a long-standing conflict between the French and English crowns over the administration of feudal lands held by English kings in France. After a period of abeyance, Henry V of England (1413–1422) renewed the conflict at the battle of Agincourt (1415) and forced the French to recognize his rights to the French throne, which he further confirmed by marrying the daughter of the king of France. After Henry's death the French monarchy under Charles VII (1422–1461), with whose name is associated the French heroine Joan of Arc, gradually began the recovery of lost lands and the expulsion of the English, goals which were not finally achieved until 1453.

b. Results of the Hundred Years' War. For France the results were disastrous: the country was ravaged, property was destroyed, large numbers of lives were lost. For England, though the war was not fought on English soil, the results were also bad; the English monarchy was weakened, society was torn by dissension, and the state was bankrupted. The most important overall effect was that nationalism in its modern form seems to have had its beginnings in the intense rivalries between the two nations. Under Louis XI (1461–1483) France began to recover and finally eliminated the menace of the duchy of Burgundy, which had consistently allied itself with England during most of the struggle. By Louis's death in 1483 France had emerged as a reunified nation with one of the strongest monarchies in Europe.

3. THE HOLY ROMAN EMPIRE

The history of the Holy Roman Empire during the Middle Ages is a story of missed opportunities. Originally intended as the medieval successor to the universal empire of Rome, it promised at one point in the tenth and eleventh centuries to become the strongest state in Europe. The long struggle with the papacy, however, and the inability of the medieval emperors to consolidate permanently the bases of their political authority kept the Holy Roman Empire from achieving its fullest potentialities. Although the emperors tried to extend their sway over other regions (most notably Italy), the medieval empire remained essentially a Germanic institution. The most important events in its medieval history were as follows: Otto I (936–973), first true Holy Roman Emperor, crowned at Rome, 962. Empire reached its peak of greatness under Henry III (1039–1056). Henry IV (1056–1106) humbled as a result of investiture controversy by Gregory VII at Canossa,

in their turn, found that the representative assemblies served as a means of limiting royal authority and protecting their own interests. Thus in many parts of Europe these representative bodies came to be serious deterrents to royal power, and the issue of sovereignty raised by this new conflict had to be settled at a later date, sometimes in favor of the crown (as in France) and sometimes in favor of the representative assembly (as in England).

Through all the vicissitudes of conflict with the church and the feudal aristocracy, monarchical power continued to expand in many parts of Europe. The most notable exception was the Holy Roman Empire, whose rulers, after a long struggle with the great feudal lords, finally sank to a position where their title was all but empty. In England and France, however, the story was very different. As a result of the Norman Conquest in 1066, English monarchs were able to reorganize the state and to make the feudal lords into tractable servants. In France this development was somewhat slower, but by the end of the thirteenth century there, too, the monarch and the royal government had triumphed. An important reason for these successes is to be found in the popularity of the monarchy. Medieval kings, by creating a central administration that dispensed justice far less partially than did the courts of the petty feudal lordlings and by giving to feudal society a stability it had previously lacked, made themselves and their governments popular with lesser men—small landholders, merchants, artisans —who had suffered from the lawlessness and caprice of feudal disorder. Above the whole of society, the king gradually came to be the symbol of an impersonal, impartial, effective state power, which, whatever its shortcomings, represented the idea of justice and the rule of law.

Ironically, the reason the two strongest monarchies of western Europe—England and France—were able to emerge as consolidated states was precisely that the papacy devoted so much of its effort for about 200 years (from the middle of the eleventh to the late thirteenth century) to winning what proved to be a hollow victory over the Holy Roman emperors. The papacy originally had much to do with the creation of the Holy Roman Empire as a secular counterpart of the church and, in theory, as the medieval heir of the long lost Roman empire of the West. For about 100 years, from the crowning of Emperor Otto I in 962 until the college of cardinals began to elect the popes on their own in 1059, popes and emperors worked together to reform the internal structure and practices of the church. As a consequence, the Holy Roman Empire, particularly in the reign of Emperor Henry III (1039–1056), grew in strength. From the point of view of ecclesiastical

1077. German penetration of Slavic lands east of Elbe river ("Drang nach Osten") begun, ca. 1130; continued by Teutonic Knights, ca. 1190–1400. Golden Bull (1356) gave seven permanent electors right to choose the emperor. Election of Albert II (1438–1439), first of the Hapsburg dynasty, which ruled the Empire until its demise (1806).

C. ECONOMIC GROWTH AND THE EXPANSION OF MEDIEVAL EUROPE, ca. 1000–1500

1. GROWTH OF URBAN LIFE

Movement for independent control of their affairs began among the towns of Italy, eleventh century. Institution of the Grand Council of Venice, 1063. Lombard League of towns defeated Emperor Frederick I (battle of Legnano), 1176.

reformers within the church, however, the growth of strong imperial power was something to be deplored because the reformers wished to rid the church of laymen's authority in matters of church appointment —that is, to do away with "lay investiture" (*see* p. 89) once and for all. In order to accomplish this, it was necessary that the ecclesiastical reformers engage *all* the monarchs of Europe in a power struggle. This struggle was most intense with the Holy Roman emperors, however, because they had previously exercised the right to nominate even the popes, and the lands of the empire included not only territories of what would later be called Germany and Austria but large parts of Italy as well. For this reason the holdings of the emperor touched and during a large part of the thirteenth century actually surrounded the lands in Italy ruled directly by the pontiffs (papal states).

The first and most spectacular success of the reformers occurred when Pope Gregory VII banned lay investiture in 1075 and in one of the dramatic confrontations of history made the ban stick by forcing the Emperor Henry IV to come to the pope at the castle of Canossa in Tuscany (January 1077) and be received as a humble penitent suing for forgiveness. The papal victory unleashed a backlash of aristocratic reaction in German lands where the great feudal magnates had looked with suspicion on growing imperial authority. As a consequence, although later emperors, most notably Frederick I (1152–1190), known to history as Frederick Barbarossa (literally, "redbeard"), and Frederick II (1211–1250), struggled to create an effective central authority within the empire, their hopes proved vain. The papacy used every stratagem as well as military force to keep the emperors' plans in check, until by the end of the thirteenth century the imperial office was an elective office with little real power. Meanwhile, however, the feudal monarchies of England and France had already laid the bases of the strong system of royal government that would make them the leading states of western Europe for centuries to come.

C. ECONOMIC GROWTH AND THE EXPANSION OF MEDIEVAL EUROPE

One of the significant and obvious developments of the modern world is the movement, usually described as "the expansion of Europe," that has seen the spread of European peoples and their civilization to every quarter of the globe. Historians customarily have thought of this expansion as beginning in the Age of Discovery from the fifteenth century onward. Conversely, they thought of the medieval period as a time

Movement spread northward as feudal monarchs granted free charters to towns: London given charter by Henry I, 1131 Formation of the north German Hanseatic League, thirteenth century. By 1500 a city like London probably had a population of about 80,000.

The pace of economic and technological change. An earlier generation of historians was wont to believe that the great changes in the techniques of European production that led to increased European wealth occurred during the course of what was sometimes called the commercial revolution of the sixteenth and seventeenth centuries. This period, they believed, was actually the time when the system commonly called capitalism—i.e., commercial and industrial production for profit—actually came into being. More recently, however, with the expansion of our knowledge of medieval economic and social history, this view has been drastically revised. It is now believed that the beginnings of European productive expansion actually occurred during the course of the tenth and eleventh centuries (ca. 950–1100). This period not only saw a rapid expansion of towns and cities but also marked the beginnings of that process of capital accumulation that was to continue intermittently throughout the history of Europe and the Western world. Down to that time the Byzantine and Arab worlds were far ahead of Latin Europe in economic development. The Byzantines and Arabs continued to maintain this lead throughout the Middle Ages; but the gap was gradually narrowed as generations passed until about 1500, when the West assumed a clear economic and technological lead, which it has never relinquished.

So far as we can now determine, this transformation was made possible by a "commercial revolution" in eleventh-century Italy, which came about because the Italians had improved production to a point where they had a surplus of commodities to sell to other Mediterranean regions. From Italy this commercial expansion spread across Europe and was paralleled by the development of a "northern trade," which encompassed north Germany, the Low Countries, northern France, and England. Improvements in business techniques (in which Italy long led the rest of Europe) and technological innovations (improvements in the use of horsepower, introduction of windmills, and increased use of waterpower) had much to do with it. Equally, if not more important, however, were changes in society itself—the development of relatively strong feudal states, the decline of violence, a rise in literacy, and the attempt to apply rationality to human affairs. All of these created a general sense of social stability and optimism, which are needed for expanding societies. This period of expansion lasted into the fourteenth century, when a period of economic and social stagnation appears to have set in from which Europe did not begin to recover until toward the end of the fifteenth century.

of economic and social stagnation in which Europe was a self-contained economic unit incapable of expansion outside its own geographical limits. But more recent research has made it plain that the Europe of the High Middle Ages was a hive of economic and technological activity wherein a great deal of internal expansion extended the local frontiers of European civilization and laid the groundwork without which the overseas expansion of a later period would have been impossible.

1. GROWTH OF URBAN LIFE

One of the more significant aspects of this internal development is to be seen in the growth of European towns and cities from the tenth century onward. Historians dispute the reasons for this urban growth, but none deny its far-reaching consequences. Economically, the rise of cities had two important long-range effects. It raised the standard of living and the economic power of important segments of the European population and thus made possible the accumulation of large amounts of fluid capital, which, by a process of continual reinvestment, ultimately made the European economic system the most dynamic the world has ever seen. Furthermore, the stimulus of intercity trade not only brought Europeans into closer contact with one another but also, as in the urban revolution of the ancient world, helped to disseminate ideas and techniques more widely than ever before. Business skills and manufacturing processes, though crude by modern standards, were extensively developed. Money came to be used widely as a medium of exchange. With these innovations, the whole of western Europe began the long process of transformation from a predominantly agricultural to a predominantly urban civilization.

In the wake of this transformation came social and political changes of great consequence. The increase in communication among the great urban centers in all parts of Europe helped to break down the localism of medieval life and in those areas where feudal kings were strong actually fostered the increase of central power. To accommodate the new cities, the social relations of feudal society had to be drastically modified. Merchants and traders needed a freedom of movement that forced a relaxation of the bonds of feudal obligation. With greater freedom the merchant became a figure of more consequence in European life. His wealth, energy, and intelligence gave him a greater political significance, with the result that his interests were more carefully considered by the state. The merchant class was not the only group affected by this transformation. The increasing needs of large centers of population required greater agricultural production; thus farming

2. RURAL LIFE, COLONIZATION, AND CONQUEST: THE CONTRACTION OF EUROPE, 1350–1450

a. Improvement in Agricultural Techniques. Development of more effective harness made possible increased utilization of horses in plowing. Mouldboard plow effectively improved preparation for crop planting. Both added significantly to medieval agricultural productivity, twelfth century. Opening up of fertile lands to which were applied new techniques in rotation and fertilization. Growth of farming surpluses and specialization of production—e.g., English wool.

b. Colonization. Continuous settlement of European border or "march" lands from the eleventh century onward. German colonists conquered the Slavs beyond the Elbe River and introduced western European agricultural techniques into the area. Settlement and partial conquest of Celtic fringe areas: English invasion and settlement of Ireland (eleventh century), conquest of Wales (thirteenth century), and attempt to conquer Scotland (fourteenth century).

c. Crusading Movements, Eleventh to Fifteenth Centuries. (1) In the Middle East. First Crusade (1099–1101) captured Jerusalem and established western feudal state in Palestine (kingdom of Jerusalem). Saladin recaptured Jerusalem (battle of Hattin), 1187. Third Crusade recaptured Acre from the Moslems, 1191. Fourth Crusade captured and sacked Constantinople, 1204. Fifth and last major Crusade captured and held Damietta (North Africa) for two years, 1219–1221. From that time forward no major effort was made to recover the Holy Land, and the West remained on the defensive against the Turks. (2) In Europe. The Order of Teutonic Knights, originally organized in the Holy Land, was invited to Prussia in 1229 to crusade against the pagan Slavs; it became a powerful social and cultural force in the Baltic region during the thirteenth and fourteenth centuries. Reconquest of Spain: defeat of the Moslems at Las Navas de Tolosa (1212) began the major phase of Christian reconquest. Ferdinand III of Castile captured Cordova (1236) and Seville (1248). Fall of Granada (1491) saw the end of the last Moslem state in Spain.

d. The Contraction of Europe, 1350–1450. Disasters struck what was, in fact, an "underdeveloped" European economy in the fourteenth century. Results (estimated): significant drop in population—e.g., in England 3.7 million people before 1346, about 2.2 million by 1377; diminution of manufacture—e.g., in Florence (Italy) textile production fell by more than 50 percent; contraction of trade—e.g., customs fees at port of Genoa (Italy) dropped 50 percent from 1293 to 1334.

was no longer pursued solely for the cultivators' subsistence but was undertaken to produce salable surpluses for city markets. Since these surpluses were usually paid for with money, many serfs and small-holders were able to buy themselves free of customary services to their feudal overlords. As this process went on, the old system of feudal-manorial relations gradually gave way to a system of greater economic and social freedom. By the sixteenth century the institution of serfdom was rapidly disappearing throughout western Europe.

2.   RURAL LIFE, COLONIZATION AND CONQUEST: THE CONTRACTION OF EUROPE, 1350–1450

As we have seen, the most important change in European rural life resulted from the growth of cities. There were other changes, however, particularly in agricultural technique and estate management, which also helped to change the social structure and to increase the wealth of Europe. As early as the twelfth century some countries were already producing specialized agricultural commodities (e.g., English wool was the focus of a specialized trade, first with Italy and then with Flanders), which enabled them to concentrate their skills in order to increase out-put. Though our evidence is scanty, the result appears to have been a rise in population and an increase in demand for land and commodities of all kinds. Largely as a result of this pressure, undeveloped lands were opened up in various parts of Europe, particularly along the bor-derlands in territories occupied by peoples like the Slavs and Celts. Elsewhere, these expansionist tendencies were reinforced by religious zeal, though it should be made plain that in many cases the religious motive was as strong or stronger than economic desire. In Spain the Moslems were pushed steadily back, until by the fourteenth century their former great holdings had all but disappeared. At the opposite end of the Mediterranean the story was somewhat different. There a series of crusades, the first launched in 1095 at papal instigation, had created the short-lived feudal kingdom of Jerusalem. In the thirteenth century Christian crusaders captured and plundered Constantinople, which for a time became a Latinized state. These eastern conquests were never permanent, however, and by the second half of the thir-teenth century only a few scattered outposts in the eastern Mediter-ranian remained in western hands.

By the beginning of the fourteenth century medieval Europe, which had enjoyed three centuries of unparalleled economic expansion, suddenly came upon bad times. The expansive trend was not just

D. MEDIEVAL CULTURE

1. MEDIEVAL PHILOSOPHY

Medieval philosophy has often been looked upon as a kind of sterile and meaningless intellectual exercise in which men only sought to prove the truth of a Christian revelation that they already accepted as a matter of faith. In one sense this judgment is true, but it fails in understanding that the philosophical accomplishments of medieval thinkers were still highly significant. The development of a rationalized Christian theology, as we noted earlier (see p. 69), is, after all, one of the unique facts about Christianity that distinguishes it from most other great world religions. What made the role of medieval thinkers significant in the development of Christianity is that certain of them, most notably Abelard and Thomas Aquinas (for both, see below), strove mightily to apply to it the processes of human reason *because* they had no wish to accept it solely on the basis of faith. Had they not undertaken to explain Christian belief in rational human terms, Christianity and indeed the whole western intellectual tradition might never have evolved along lines later taken by both. The long debate over the problem of universals, for example, well illustrates the nature of their intellectual striving. In the argument as to whether the general concepts in our minds such as truth, justice, beauty, God, church, and state have real existence outside our minds, these thinkers were examining one of the most persistent questions of western philosophy, which is with us even today. One school of thought approved by the church, the "realists," believed that

stopped; for about fifty years it was actually reversed so significantly that large areas of the continent did not begin to recover until about 1450. The cause was a combination of calamities that must be regarded as almost unexampled historic misfortunes. The first of them was a famine that seriously diminished or completely wiped out agricultural surpluses in many parts of Europe. A second calamity consisted of a succession of devastating wars involving the Turks and Christians in southeastern Europe; Germans and Lithuanians in the Baltic region; and, worst of all, the protracted intermittent struggle between England and France, from 1336 to 1453, which is known as the Hundred Years' War. Even more dramatic were the great plagues that visited the continent at intervals throughout the century—1346–1350, 1360–1363, 1371–1374, 1381–1384—after an absence of nearly 600 years. While the evidence is scattered, it seems plain that many parts of Europe suffered serious population loss, particularly following the most famous of the plagues, the Black Death of 1346–1350.

D.   MEDIEVAL CULTURE

As it was with medieval economic expansion, so it was with medieval culture. Despite the pervasive authority of the church and its system of theology that provided answers, in broad outline, to all the "big questions" about man and his place in the universe, the intellectual activity of medieval men was neither so arid nor as futile as it has sometimes seemed. It is true that the Middle Ages did not reach a high level of scientific achievement and that there were real limitations to human speculation. But, in spite of these, medieval thinkers made notable contributions to human knowledge in an atmosphere of freedom no more restricted than that of some twentieth-century societies.

1.   MEDIEVAL PHILOSOPHY

In the field of philosophy the greatest accomplishment of the Middle Ages was its completion of the process by which the learning of antiquity was finally incorporated into Christian thought. This work of incorporation had been going forward since the days of the early church fathers, but in the thirteenth century it culminated in the absorption by the Christian West of the whole body of Aristotle's writings. The accomplishment was by no means easy, for there had been continuous resistance over the centuries to every attempt on the part of Christian scholars to make use of what were called "profane" writings. The truth of Christianity, it was asserted by enemies of secular learning, had been revealed in scripture and the traditions of the

such concepts did have a "real" existence. Their opponents, known as "nominalists," believed that all general ideas (mankind, for example) have reality only because we know about particulars (individual men). They did not solve the problem, but by their very discussion of it they helped to make close rational inquiry concerning the process of knowing an important part of the western tradition.

Saint Anselm of Bec and Canterbury (1034?–1109) offered his "one sentence" proof of the existence of God arrived at by logical method.

Abelard (1079–1142) in his *Sic et Non* (Yes or No?) applied reason to the writings of the church fathers in order to prove the truth of the Christian faith; his effort was condemned by the church.

Gradual recovery of the works of Aristotle (Aristotelian *corpus*), particulary after the reconquest of Toledo (Spain) in 1085, led to attempts to incorporate his writings into Christian thought.

Albertus Magnus (Saint Albert the Great), 1206–1280, collected and commented upon Aristotle's works.

Saint Thomas Aquinas, 1225–1274, incorporated Aristotelian knowledge into Christian theology *(Summa Theologica)*.

2. RISE OF THE UNIVERSITIES

Since many of the universities evolved out of earlier monastic or cathedral schools, it is difficult to say just when the first of them came into existence. Many of them began as scholastic guilds—that is, spontaneous unions of teachers and students. Among the earlier and more famous of the university foundations were Salerno in Italy, tenth to eleventh centuries; Bologna, eleventh century; Paris (the most famous of the medieval universities), 1150–1170; Oxford, late twelfth century; and Cambridge, early thirteenth century.

3. MEDIEVAL LITERATURE AND ART

a. Literature. Heroic epic (*Beowulf* and the *Nibelungenlied*) constituted the major literary form before 1100; largely folk inspired. About the eleventh century three new forms appeared: (1) the *chansons de geste*, like the *Song of Roland*, which were tales of heroic deeds; (2) the poetry of the troubadours, which dealt with chivalry, courtesy, and courtly love; and (3) the great poetic legends like the Arthurian and Grail legends, which reflected strong Christian influences. In the later Middle Ages, particularly in the fourteenth century, poems of social criticism appeared. Among the best known of these was William Langland's *Vision of Piers Plowman*. Better known, though it is something more than a work of social criticism, is Geoffrey Chaucer's (1340–1400) *Canterbury Tales*. The most popular

church. Since these were all-sufficient for human salvation, there was little need to delve into studies that were irrelevant to the great task of preparing men for a life immortal. If medieval philosophies had really been so completely lacking in intellectual curiosity or so restricted in their outlook as is sometimes said, they would have been content to accept this judgment and let the matter rest. But they were not, and therein lay the greatness of their achievement.

By the late twelfth century an intellectual crisis was reached when the works of Aristotle, translated from Arab sources, began to make their way into western Europe. Within a few decades of their appearance heretical opinions, evidently stimulated by the new ideas, began to be expressed in many centers of learning, particularly at the University of Paris; and church authorities moved quickly to suppress the dangerous Aristotelian writings. But two great scholar-philosophers now came forward to undertake the difficult task of assimilating Aristotle without, at the same time, creating heresies. Albertus Magnus (d. 1280) and Thomas Aquinas (1225–1274) between them accomplished the collection and indexing of Aristotle's thought and its recasting in Christian terms. When the work of Aquinas (*Summa Theologica*) was completed, it was immediately accepted by the church and became a central part of medieval Christian theology. Later this adoption of Aristotle was to have a stultifying effect on the development of scientific and other thought, because Aristotelian learning came to be accepted too slavishly. Ultimately, however, the preservation of Greek philosophy within the Christian tradition helped the intellectual development of the West even more than it hindered, for the Aristotelian system assumed the existence of an ordered universe explainable in rational terms. This assumption, when linked with empirical method, helped forge the intellectual tools of modern science.

2. THE RISE OF THE UNIVERSITIES

Perhaps the most original contribution of the medieval world to modern cultural development was the specialized center of advanced studies known as the university. Schools of philosophy had existed in ancient Athens, and something like them had been revived in the days of Charlemagne. Throughout the early Middle Ages, however, monasteries and abbeys had undertaken to impart a knowledge of advanced subjects if there happened to be a distinguished scholar or group of scholars attached to a particular monastic center. In the twelfth century there grew up a number of schools attached to great cathedrals, probably as results of the growing need for men with intellectual training for the administrative posts of the church and of the rise in intellectual

medieval poem was *The Romance of the Rose*, the first part of which was written by William de Lorris (thirteenth century). The work was a long ingenious love poem that combined pagan allegory with Christian ideals. The greatest of medieval poems, *The Divine Comedy* of Dante Alighieri (1265–1321), is a wonderful combination of art and reason. Dante summarized the thought of his own time within a literary framework of great beauty, a combination achieved by only a few great writers.

b. Medieval Art. Medieval architecture, more than any other art form, reflected the dominant religious tone of the age. Gothic cathedrals were cooperative enterprises that required the work of many hands for generations. The Gothic style, which originated in northern France during the twelfth century, was characterized by the pointed arch and vault, which made it possible to rest the ceiling and roof upon a relatively small number of slender columns and buttresses rather than upon massive continuous walls; the space in the resultant skeleton wall could be filled with broad expanses of stained glass, with the result that the Gothic church interior was always filled with light of various hues; the stone surfaces, wherever men could reach, were covered with traceries and carvings.

standards following the ecclesiastical reforms of the tenth and eleventh centuries. These schools tended to attract students from all over Europe and in time were organized into university corporations. The course of studies followed a formalized pattern leading ultimately to degrees in the liberal arts, theology, law, or medicine. During the thirteenth century the University of Paris was the most famous of these new centers of learning and set the model for other university foundations—including Oxford and Cambridge—throughout the north of Europe. The vigor of late medieval intellectual life may best be seen in the fact that by the end of the Middle Ages some 80 universities had come into existence in all parts of Europe, from Cracow in the East to Lisbon in the West and from Upsala in Sweden to Catania in Sicily.

3. MEDIEVAL LITERATURE AND ART

Medieval literature, despite the otherworldliness of the age and the influence of religious themes, was extremely varied. Great epic poems like the Anglo-Saxon *Beowulf* and the French *Song of Roland*, as well as the chivalric poetry of the troubadours and the *Arthurian Legend*, attest to the vitality of medieval literary expression. Perhaps its greatest single production is to be found in that massive combination of art and intellect, *The Divine Comedy* of Dante (1265–1321), which represents one of the most successful efforts ever made to combine the whole body of thought of a particular period with a narrative of surpassing artistry. The other great artistic contribution of medieval men was Gothic architecture. Originating in northern France, it reached its peak in the twelfth and thirteenth centuries with great cathedrals whose stone tracery and stained-glass windows combined to give unity to an art form that was intended to be a perfect manifestation of esthetics and religious faith.

chapter seven

EVENTS AND DEFINITIONS

The setbacks—famine, plague, local losses in population, wars and decline of trade—of the fourteenth century, though serious, did not put a stop to the long-range economic and social expansion of Europe. If anything, the process of expansion that occurred during most of the High Middle Ages was slowed only for two or three generations. By the middle of the fifteenth century the Atlantic states of Europe—Spain, Portugal, England, France, and Holland—were creating wealth and skills that would make it possible for Europeans in significant numbers to move outward from their own shores to all parts of the world. During this same period parts of the Italian peninsula were to pass through a time of intense economic and artistic creativity, which historians have for long designated as the Renaissance.

Renaissance and Reformation

THE ESSENTIAL MOVEMENT

The terms "Renaissance" and "Reformation" have been used for so long to describe certain definite periods of European history that it is difficult to think of any others to take their places. Yet to some extent, both are misnomers.

The word "renaissance" means rebirth; when used to describe Europe in the fourteenth, fifteenth and sixteenth centuries, "renaissance" implies that the history of the Middle Ages was of little relative importance, socially or culturally. Since we know that the medieval period was far more productive and original than was once believed, the period of the Renaissance has now come to be thought of not as a sharp break with the medieval past but, rather, as a time when many movements and ideas originating in the Middle Ages came to fruition. The Renaissance was thus not so much a time of rebirth as of shifting emphasis, a time when the tempo of human activity quickened and men thought more explicitly about things of this world without reference to the hereafter or without allowing themselves to be quite so influenced by the traditional standards of Christian belief as they had been previously.

A. THE RENAISSANCE, ca. 1400–1600

1. ECONOMIC AND SOCIAL CHANGE

a. Use of New Financial Techniques. ˙Bills of exchange (drafts calling for the payment of sums of money by one merchant in behalf of another), promissory notes, and discounting (deducting of charges for interest in advance from loans), which greatly expanded credit and eased the transfer of wealth, began to be used extensively from the fourteenth century onward. Earliest public banks created in the early fifteenth century. Stock and monetary exchanges (bourses) were established, the most famous of which was founded at Antwerp, 1531.

b. Development of Business Organization. Double-entry system of bookkeeping in use as early as the fourteenth century. Permanent business partnerships, group organizations to share insurance risks, and, finally, the joint-stock company evolved from the fourteenth through the seventeenth centuries.

In somewhat the same way our understanding of the term "reformation," as used to describe the period of religious struggle in the sixteenth century, has also changed. When the division between Catholics and Protestants first occurred, the religious leaders who broke away from the medieval church thought of themselves as "reformers," whose purpose was to eliminate the abuses in the church that, as they saw it, had grown up during the long centuries of papal supremacy. In most cases, they wished not to create something new or to destroy the unity of Christendom by founding numerous sects and denominations but rather to restore the church as it had been founded by Christ and the apostles. For this reason they were driven to appeal to the authority of the Bible as against the authority of the popes and the historical traditions of the church. But because the language of the Scriptures is in many places ambiguous or even contradictory, they found themselves in disagreement, not only with the medieval church but also among themselves. As a consequence, the great Protestant hope of reforming and preserving a united Christian church was never achieved. The medieval church (thenceforward to be known as the Roman Catholic church) continued to exist side by side with the various new Protestant denominations; and the Reformation, with time, took on the aspects not of a reform movement but of a religious revolution with far-reaching significance.

A. THE RENAISSANCE

1. ECONOMIC AND SOCIAL CHANGES

By the midfifteenth century the revived forces of economic expansion began to produce a higher level of material well-being, particularly in the great European cities. At first this increase in wealth was most noticeable in the Italian peninsula and the Low Countries (now Belgium and Holland), but in time it spread rapidly to other parts of northern and western Europe. As it spread, it created a new, sophisticated mercantile civilization, outstanding examples of which were the great city-states: Venice, Genoa, Florence, Milan in Italy; Antwerp, Bruges, and Ghent in the Low Countries; and the towns of the Hanseatic League in north central Germany. The most brilliant manifestations of this new civilization were in Italy, where the continuity of city life from Roman times onward had never been completely broken. In the Italian cities great merchant families made use of their wealth to promote learning and the arts. In so doing, however, they seldom lost sight of the practi-

c.   The Mercantile Recovery of Europe.   From the end of the fourteenth century an increase in commercial activity, an accumulation of capital wealth, and a greater sophistication in business skills steadily undermined the church's traditional ethical teachings, which prohibited the taking of interest on loans (usury) and selling at more than a "just price." In part, this was a reflection of the growing interest in things of this world, of a desire for well-being in the here and now rather than awaiting reward in the hereafter. With the spread of this attitude and an increasing accumulation of commercial and financial wealth, great merchants and financiers became important figures.

d.   New Men of Wealth.   Three outstanding members of the new financial-mercantile class were: (1) Giovanni dei Medici (1360–1429), merchant and banker of Florence, who founded the powerful Medici family. His descendants later became princes and popes. (2) Jacques Coeur (ca. 1395–1456), merchant of Bourges in France, possessed the largest fortune ever amassed by a private individual in France down to his time. Friend, confidant, and adviser to French kings. (3) The Fugger family in Germany began to increase wealth at the end of the fourteenth century. By the sixteenth century its members were the wealthiest men in Europe, one of whom supplied the vast sums needed to carry the imperial election of 1519 in favor of Charles of Hapsburg.

2.   THE GREAT DISCOVERIES

a.   Causes.   (1) Growth of wealth, which made expensive and risky overseas ventures possible; (2) religious and national zeal; (3) desire for gain; (4) effort of some religious minorities to escape persecution; (5) curiosity and the simple desire to increase knowledge; and, finally, (6) the development of a technology that made long oceanic voyages possible (compass, sternpost rudder, seaworthy construction of ships, improved methods of celestial navigation).

b.   Chronology of Discovery and Settlement to 1620.   Journeys of Marco Polo to the Far East, 1271–1295. Prince Henry the Navigator of Portugal began to promote voyages of discovery along the African coast, 1418. Discovery of the Azores, 1427–1431, and Cape Verde Islands, 1455–1457. Diaz rounded the Cape of Good Hope, 1487–1488. First voyage of Columbus, 1492. Vasco da Gama sailed to India, 1497–1499. Cabot brothers touched the coast of North America, 1497–1498. Balboa discovered Pacific, 1513. Conquest of Mexico by Cortez, 1519–1521. Conquest of Peru by Pizarro, 1532–1533. First English circumnavigation of the globe by Drake, 1577–1580. Beginning of Dutch trade with the East Indies, 1595–1597. Founding of the English East India Company, 1600; of the Dutch East India Company, 1602.

cal side of their affairs; in these Italian merchant communities were developed many of the business skills that were later used internationally. For the first time there appeared on the European scene the great financier, whose wealth made him the creditor of kings and gave him a power (sometimes exaggerated by later historians) to influence political decisions.

The Renaissance also saw the completion of the process of state development begun by medieval kings. Curiously enough, the areas most affected by this change—England, France, and Spain—were not the first to feel the effects of the quickened economic and intellectual tempo. It was in Italy that the new spirit first appeared, but there the Renaissance was a period of political chaos when city fought city and foreign powers intervened to carve out Italian possessions for themselves. In England, France, and Spain, however, the end of the fifteenth and the beginning of the sixteenth centuries saw the emergence of three strong dynasties (Tudors in England, Valois in France, Hapsburgs in Spain) who greatly increased the power of their respective governments and virtually eliminated the last vestiges of feudal opposition. With the rise of these new states the center of European power shifted to the Atlantic fringe, and a new era—the age of the absolute monarchies—had begun.

2. THE GREAT DISCOVERIES

While important internal changes were taking place in the fifteenth and sixteenth centuries, another series of events decisively altered the relations of Europe with the rest of the world and led ultimately to Europe's becoming the center of a worldwide cultural and economic community. These were the great discoveries beyond the seas. Columbus's famous voyage was but one of many, though perhaps the most sensational of them. The discoveries, and the colonization movements that followed in their wake, were the further result of a number of medieval and Renaissance developments: (1) the internal expansion of European wealth, which made it possible to finance costly voyages and to undertake extensive colonization programs; (2) advances in shipbuilding techniques; (3) improvement in the methods of economic and political organization—e.g., the joint-stock company, which made possible the sharing of great economic risks, and the strong centralized state, which enabled European rulers to give sanction and support to overseas activities; and (4) the growth and improvement of communication within Europe, which stimulated interest in remote territories. The motives that drove Europeans to undertake the risks of discovery and exploration were varied. Many were driven by hope of sudden

English settlement in North America (Jamestown), 1607. Founding of French Canada (Québec) by Champlain, 1608. Establishment of the English in India, 1609–1614. Voyage of the *Mayflower*; second permanent English settlement in North America, 1620–1621.

3. LITERATURE AND THOUGHT

a. In Italy. *Divine Comedy*, written between 1300 and 1311, reflected the ideals of the thirteenth century and also foreshadowed the future, since it was written in the vernacular (Italian rather than Latin). The writings of Petrarch (1304–1374) characterized the change; topics chosen were secular in interest. Publication of Boccaccio's *Decameron*, 1353. Founding of the humanist school at Mantua, 1425. Marsilio Ficino became head of the Platonic Academy (whose members opposed the Aristotelian influences of the medieval schoolmen) at Florence, 1458. Rule of Lorenzo de Medici ("the Magnificent") in Florence, 1469–1492. Appearance of Machiavelli's *The Prince*, 1515.

b. Outside Italy. Publication of the first part of Cervantes' *Don Quixote* (Spain), 1505. Erasmus' *In Praise of Folly* (1509) satirized contemporary ills, particularly those of the church. Thomas More's *Utopia*, 1516. Foundation of the Collège de France (1530) which became the center of French humanism. Rabelais' *Gargantua and Pantagruel*, 1532. Andreas Vesalius published *Seven Books on the Structure of the Human Body*, 1543. Appearance of Copernicus's *De revolutionibis orbium coelestium (On the Revolution of Celestial Bodies)*, 1543. Shakespeare's first plays appeared, 1590–1594. Publication of the first part of Edmund Spenser's *The Faerie Queene*, 1590.

4. RENAISSANCE ART

a. In Italy. Giotto's frescoes at Padua, 1305. Botticelli painted "Birth of Venus," 1485. Leonardo da Vinci's "Last Supper" painted 1485–1498. Construction began on the basilica of St. Peter's (Rome), 1506. *School of Athens*

wealth or by the desire to open new trade routes. Some hoped to Christianize the pagans or, later, to escape from religious persecution at home. Kings were moved by considerations of power and prestige. All, however, were impelled by some form of the restless human vitality and curiosity that has been so marked a characteristic of modern European civilization.

3. LITERATURE AND THOUGHT

In the literary movements of the Renaissance two distinctive features emerged. The first of these was the tendency, already evident in Dante's *Divine Comedy* (though, as we have seen, its content was purely medieval), to make use of the native (vernacular) languages rather than medieval Latin as a medium of expression. This change, though it did open the way to a broadening of interests and tastes, was not all gain, for it resulted in the decline of an international language that had helped to unify western Christendom. The second distinctive feature of the new literature was its emphasis on man and man's place in this world (humanism), stimulated by an interest in the writings of classical antiquity. Because many of the leading literary figures of the early Renaissance, men like the poet-scholar Petrarch (1304–1374), wished to return to the grammatical purity of classical Latin that medieval Latin had lost, it later came to be assumed that medieval scholars had known nothing of the great literary works of antiquity and that the Renaissance scholars, by rediscovering them, had ushered in an age of "rebirth." The claim was an exaggeration, but it was not entirely without meaning, for Renaissance scholars and thinkers did help to shift both the intellectual and literary interests of the time from Christian to classical or secular subjects. With this shift a great number of thinkers began to concern themselves with man in the world of here and now. Our best illustration of this new tendency is to be found in the writings of that tough-minded realist, Niccolo Machiavelli (1469–1527), whose political writings—the most famous of which was *The Prince*—helped to divorce political theory from Christian morality. At the other extreme, however, was the Dutch humanist scholar Erasmus (1466–1536), whose breadth of knowledge led him to exalt human values but not to separate them from the traditional ethics.

4. RENAISSANCE ART

The art of the Renaissance also reflects the change in emphasis characteristic of its literature and thought. Whereas architecture, as seen in the great Gothic cathedrals, had been the highest artistic achievement

and *Disputa* painted by Raphael, 1509–1511. Painting of Michelangelo's *Last Judgment*, 1534–1541. Death of Titian, 1576.

b. Outside Italy. Albrecht Dürer's woodcuts on *The Revelation of St. John* (Germany), 1498. Hans Holbein the Younger settled in England, 1532. Philibert Delorme published French manual of architecture, 1561. Escorial Palace built by Philip II of Spain at Madrid, 1563–1584. Death of El Greco, 1625, greatest Spanish painter of the Renaissance.

B. THE REFORMATION

John Wyclif (1320–1384) of England attacked the theology of the medieval church 1378–1380; Wyclif's followers, known as Lollards, suppressed by King Henry IV (1399–1413). Great schism of the church finally healed by Council of Constance; same council also executed the Bohemian John Hus for heresy, 1415. Restoration of papal unity with election of Martin V, 1417. Hussite Wars in Bohemia, 1420–1433. Conciliar movement, which threatened papal authority, finally lost out in struggle with papacy when Council of Basel, 1431–1449, failed in its attempt to make a representative council the governing body of the church. Decline of the Renaissance papacy: pontificate of the humanist pope, Nicholas V, 1447–1455; Alexander VI (Borgia), 1492–1503. Establishment of the Spanish Inquisition, 1478. Savonarola preached against clerical abuses at Florence, 1494–1498. Humanist criticism of clerical abuses: *In Praise of Folly* by Erasmus, 1509; *Utopia* by Sir Thomas More, 1516; *The Letters of Obscure Men* by Rubeanus and Ulrich von Hutten, 1515–1517.

Influence of Humanism on the Reformation. Although humanist criticism had much to do with preparing the climate of opinion that made the Reformation possible, humanism and Protestantism were separate and distinct movements. Humanist critics, particularly in northern Europe, were not anti-Christian or even opposed to the medieval church as it was constituted about 1500. Most of them, when the crisis of the Reformation came, remained within the church. Their writings and attitudes, however, inadvertently made men aware of the church's shortcomings in the early sixteenth century. Concordat of Bologna between papacy and Francis I of France gave the king virtual control of the French church; publication of new Greek edition of the New Testament by Erasmus; indulgence mission of Tetzel to Germany, 1516. Reign of the Emperor Charles V, 1519–1556.

of medieval man, the Renaissance artist turned his attention to such individual forms of art as painting and sculpture. As a consequence of a revolution in artistic method, the new artist was able to portray his subjects with a natural exactness and a richness of detail that had been lacking in medieval art; and while he still chose religious themes for expression, he also chose many that were nonreligious. The growth of artistic naturalism may be traced from its beginnings in Giotto's (ca. 1270–1337) paintings through the pictures and sculpture of such great figures as Leonardo da Vinci (1452–1519), Michelangelo (1475–1564), and Titian (1477—1576), whose work typifies the new diversity and variety of a vastly enriched artistic medium.

B. THE REFORMATION

When we look for the general causes of the great religious split between Catholics and Protestants, which began with Martin Luther (1483–1546) in the first quarter of the sixteenth century, we find two kinds.

The first type of cause arose from the great changes in the attitude of men toward the world in which they lived, which had occurred during the fourteenth, fifteenth, and sixteenth centuries. These changes were bound to make many persons resentful of an authority like that of the medieval church, which professed to be universal and supernational. Kings and nobles disliked the moral curbs placed on them by the church's teaching and looked with disfavor and envy on the growing wealth and the administrative bureaucracy of such a powerful organization. Merchants were restive at the traditional prohibitions of canon law against the taking of interest on loans and against other business practices that are now accepted as normal and honorable, even though these prohibitions had declined in force during the late Middle Ages. Moreover, with the rise of strong monarchies and the growth of a sense of national distinctiveness, it was difficult for many Europeans to think of the papacy as anything other than an Italian institution that drew taxes from them to serve its own ends. In the face of these growing forces of secular discontent, some sort of break with papal authority might well have come without a Martin Luther to lead it. Attitudes had changed and the changes led men more and more to a rejection of the church's spiritual teachings.

The second variety of general cause of the Reformation lay in the Renaissance church itself, which gave Luther and other Protestants something to criticize and thus helped to create the upheaval that fol-

1. LUTHERANISM

Luther's life: born at Eisleben, 1483. Studied at University of Erfurt whose
leading theologian, Gabriel Biel (d. 1495), was under the influence of the
"nominalist" philosopher William of Ockham (ca. 1300–1349). Like most
Ockhamists, Luther believed in the separation of reason and faith. Entered
the order of Augustinian Eremites, 1505; ordained priest, 1507. Visited
Rome, 1510–1511, and taught at Wittenberg after 1512. Gradually came to
conclusion that man is "justified by faith alone," 1512–1517. In reaction
to the Tetzel indulgence mission published his 95 Theses, 1517. Excommunicated by Pope Leo X, 1520. Defied Emperor Charles V at Diet of Worms,
1521. Took the side of the princes in suppressing Peasants' Revolt, 1524–
1525. Later history of Lutheranism: Augsburg Confession (*Confessio
Augustana*) set forth principles of Lutheran belief, 1531. National Protestant
(Lutheran) church established in Sweden, 1527; in Denmark, 1536. Death of
Luther, 1546. Lutheran-Catholic religious wars (1546–1555) culminated in
Peace of Augsberg, 1555, which recognized Lutheranism; permitted princes
to determine which faith would prevail in their territories ("cuius regio,
eius religio").

2. CALVINISM

Translation of the Bible into French, 1523–1530. Calvin converted to
Protestantism and fled Paris, 1533. Publication of Calvin's *Institutes of the
Christian Religion*, 1536. Founding of theocratic Calvinist state at Geneva,
1541. British exiles carry Calvinist ideas to England (after the accession of
Elizabeth I in 1558) and Scotland (John Knox returned in 1559). Scottish
Parliament severed ties with Rome, 1560. Death of Calvin, 1564. Revolt of
the Netherlands begun in part under Calvinist auspices, 1566. Declaration of

lowed. For the fact was that some of the churchmen, though by no means all or even a majority, had succumbed to the secular influences of the age. Ecclesiastical discipline and morality had become lax in many places, and, worse, some of the Renaissance popes themselves were guilty of flagrant abuses of their high office. Thus a combination of discontents came into existence, some aroused by secular feelings and others by a fear that the church, through certain of its practices, was placing the salvation of thousands of human beings in jeopardy. For men like Martin Luther and John Calvin (1509–1564), who were destined to become the two leading figures of the Protestant movement, the latter issue was by far the most important. Though there were men who would follow their lead for selfish, material reasons, these two acted on the high religious purpose of restoring the church of the apostles.

1.   LUTHERANISM

In 1517 Luther initiated the religious revolt in Germany with a public challenge (Ninety-five Theses) to debate certain propositions that struck at the heart of the prevailing theology of the church and implicitly questioned papal authority. His challenge struck a chord of popular response and within a few years had led to his expulsion from the church. What made it possible for Luther to succeed where earlier religious leaders had failed was the decision on the part of certain territorial princes and nobles to back him in his struggle. This support left the lands of the Holy Roman Empire divided into two armed camps. On one side were the Lutheran nobles and on the other Emperor Charles V (1519–1556), who remained loyal to the Roman Catholic church. After a period of protracted warfare in which the two sides fought each other to a standstill, the Peace of Augsburg (1555) effected a compromise by allowing local princes to determine what the religions of their territories would be. With this adjustment, Protestantism became a permanent part of the European historical tradition.

2.   CALVINISM

While Lutheranism spread throughout north Germany and into Scandinavia, elsewhere in Europe a new and equally strong protest movement was taking shape. In Switzerland, where the religious leader Ulrich Zwingli had begun the revolt of 1524, a new and powerful personality—John Calvin, a French preacher of the new doctrines who had fled to the city of Geneva in 1536—undertook to organize the church that afterwards bore his name. The distinctiveness of the Calvinist

Dutch independence from Spain, 1581. Religious Wars in France (Catholics against the Calvinist Huguenots), 1563–1598: massacre of St. Bartholomew wiped out important French Huguenot leaders, 1572; Henry IV became Catholic convert from Calvinism, 1593, and issued the Edict of Nantes granting toleration to Huguenots, 1598.

Essentially, the theological position of Calvin, like that of Luther, stressed the importance of faith as opposed to good works in attaining salvation. Because certain of Calvin's writings seemed to stress the role of faith so exclusively, it has been believed that Calvinism was a religion of predestination (i.e., a theology that believes that God "predestines" or predetermines who shall be saved and who shall be damned and that men have no control over their own ultimate destinies). Such a view quite clearly implies that men are not ultimately responsible for their actions, no matter how unethical. Calvin did not, in fact, relieve men of all responsibility for their sins, as some of his critics have implied. Nevertheless, he emphasized the omnipotence of God in controlling the universe and the fate of men. It is for this reason that many people have thought of Calvinism as a stern, unbending faith in which divine authority is stressed at the expense of divine love.

3. ANGLICANISM

Henry VIII (1509–1547) summoned the Reformation Parliament, 1529. Henry divorced Catherine of Aragon and married Anne Boleyn, 1533; Pope Clement VII excommunicated Henry. Henry proclaimed head of the Church of England, 1534. Dissolution of the monasteries, 1536–1539. Protestant reforms pushed under Edward VI (1547–1553); first English Book of Common Prayer published, 1549. Catholicism restored during the reign of Queen Mary, 1553–1558. Queen Elizabeth I (1558–1603) established Anglican church: Act of Supremacy, 1559, recognized queen's control of the church, and in the same year the Act of Uniformity ordered Englishmen to conform to the new ceremonies. Thirty-nine Articles (1563) defined the theology of the Church of England.

English Puritans began to protest against vestiges of medieval customs in the English Church after 1566. Richard Hooker wrote the *Laws of Ecclesiastical Polity*, which defined the theological position of Anglicanism, 1594–1601. James I (1603–1625) rejected Puritan demands for reform at Hampton Court Conference, 1604.

church organization lay in the fact that it allowed the laity to participate in church functions as members of the governing body known as the "presbytery." Above the presbytery was a hierarchy of graded courts which undertook the surveillance of public morality with far greater efficiency than any of the courts of the medieval church had possessed. From the outset Calvin made it plain that his movement was intended to supplant the medieval church, to become, in other words, the universal, "reformed" church of Christendom. Impelled by this purpose, Calvinism spread rapidly into France, the Low Countries, the Holy Roman Empire, Scotland, and England. Wherever it appeared, the militancy of its adherents frequently led to conflicts with the existing authority and in some countries to bitter wars of religion.

3. ANGLICANISM

Anglican Protestantism, the branch of the new movement that developed the English state church, differed from Lutheranism and Calvinism in that the original leadership of the revolt did not come from a great religious leader (though many prominent churchmen gave it their support) but from the state. King Henry VIII (1509–1547) broke with papal authority and proclaimed himself head of the Church of England in 1534. His motives were complex—personal, political, dynastic, patriotic, and vaguely reformist. At first, this break took the form of a schism (separation) in which all the forms, ceremonies, and much of the theology of the medieval church were preserved. Gradually, however, as Henry moved to abolish the monasteries and to introduce other changes, the English church became more and more Protestant. In the reign of Edward VI (1547–1553) the Protestantizing of the church was accelerated with such success that the efforts of the Catholic queen Mary (1553–1558) to restore England to her own faith proved unavailing. With the accession of Elizabeth I (1558–1603) the form of the Anglican church was finally settled by a compromise in which the organization of the medieval church was retained but the theology of continental Protestantism became the basis of doctrinal belief. Unfortunately, though many Englishmen were satisfied with this middle-of-the-road position, others were not, and this discontent sowed the seeds

4. THE CATHOLIC REFORMATION

Founding of the Theatine (1524) and Capuchin (1525–1528) orders for the purpose of reforming clerical life. Society of Jesus (Jesuits) organized by Ignatius Loyola (1534); recognized by the pope, 1540. The order was intended through its militancy and discipline to win back Protestants and to combat heresy. Council of Trent reaffirmed the doctrinal position of the church and pronounced the various Protestant theologies to be heresies; undertook extensive reforms in clerical life, 1545–1563. Reform of the Roman curia (central governing body of the Catholic Church) by Pope Paul IV, 1555–1559. Index of prohibited books established, 1557.

The theological position of the church, which was confirmed at the Council of Trent, came to be known as the Tridentine Faith (after the Latin name for Trent). In essence, the theologians of Trent reaffirmed the church's central position that both "faith" and "works" were needed for salvation and that what seemed to be the Protestant stress on faith alone was to be rejected completely. The council also confirmed the church's traditional teachings on the supremacy of the papacy, the ritual of the mass, and the dogma of transubstantiation (belief that the bread and wine of communion become the real body and blood of Christ at the moment of priestly consecration). By this decision all possibility of theological compromise with Protestantism was at an end.

5. THE HISTORICAL SIGNIFICANCE OF PROTESTANTISM

a. Major Religious Divisions of Europe after the Reformation. ("E" in parentheses denotes established or official state churches.)

1. Lutheran: In North Germany Hesse (E), Saxony (E), Brandenberg (Prussia) (E), and Württemberg (E). In Scandinavia Denmark (E), Norway (E), Sweden (E), and Finland (E).
2. Calvinist: Rhenish Palatinate (E), parts of Hungary and Poland, regions of western and southwestern France, parts of north Germany, the

of later trouble. Catholics disliked the Church of England's theology and its denial of papal authority, whereas the Puritans, a new group so known from their wish to "purify" the church, were angry at its retention of certain Catholic elements. In spite of these difficulties the Anglican church, because it was purposely broad and comprehensive in its doctrines, was able to include in its membership the great body of loyal Englishmen. In this way it became the prototype of the new kind of national church that sprang up all over Europe in the wake of the Reformation.

4. THE CATHOLIC REFORMATION

In the face of growing religious unrest, which by the middle of the sixteenth century threatened to destroy the medieval church completely, a series of movements was begun within the Catholic church to strengthen its organization and to eliminate some of the problems that had brought on the Protestant revolt. Moves to counter the various outbreaks of religious rebellion sometimes took the form of repression. The Inquisition, a special administrative body originally organized in the Middle Ages for the examination of heretics, was given wide powers, particularly in Spain and Italy; and the support of Catholic kings and nobles was solicited to prevent the further spread of heresy. The greatest successes of the church, however, were achieved as a result of a spiritual rejuvenation in which the Society of Jesus (Jesuits), founded in 1540 by the soldier-saint Ignatius Loyola (1491–1556), took the lead. By stressing discipline, loyalty to the papacy, and a firm adherence to both religious principles and intellectual standards, the Jesuits were able to keep and to win back countless numbers for the church. In the climax a great church council held at Trent in Italy (1545–1563) reaffirmed the doctrinal teachings of the church; and while this orthodox body prevented any final reconciliation with the Protestants, it reformed numerous things that had been complained of and restored the high standards of Catholic clerical life.

5. THE HISTORICAL SIGNIFICANCE OF PROTESTANTISM

Protestantism has sometimes been looked upon by historians as the source of many such modern developments as capitalism, liberalism, democracy, and nationalism. In the main, this conclusion has derived from the belief that Protestantism, and particularly Calvinism, by its stress on scriptural authority and through its theology, opened the way to a philosophy of individualism that greatly influenced modern economic and political thinking. This view is sound only if we look at

Netherlands (E), Scotland (E), parts of England, northern Ireland, Geneva (E), and parts of Switzerland.
3. Anglican: England and Wales (E); established church in Ireland though the great majority of the population remained Catholic.
4. Roman Catholic: Poland, most of Hungary, south Germany. Austria, France, Spain, Portugal, and the Italian peninsula. Where the Roman · Catholic Church survived it was invariably the established church.

b. Other Religious Movements.
1. English Puritanism originated ca. 1566 as a movement to "purify" the Church of England.
2. Socinianism, forerunner of later Unitarianism, founded by Laelius (1525–1562) and Faustus (1539–1604) Socinus (Sozzini), two sixteenth-century Italian reformers.
3. Separatism: term applied to those English Puritan groups after 1588 that wished to separate from the Church of England rather than to reform it from within.
4. Arminianism: movement within Calvinism named for the Dutch theologian Jacobus Arminius (1560–1609) who sought to mitigate the extreme predestinarian theories of orthodox Calvinism.
5. Jansenism: mainly a French movement within the Roman Catholic Church that, like orthodox Calvinism, tended to stress predestination. Took its name from the Dutch Catholic theologian, Bishop Cornelis Jansen (1585–1638), whose posthumous work *Augustinus* (1643) became the theological basis of the movement.
6. English-speaking denominationalism: one of the extraordinary characteristics of English Protestantism was its tendency to divide into numerous denominations. Among the more famous of these were: the Independents (Congregationalists), whose leading members were

certain indirect effects of Protestant thought. Both Luther and Calvin rejected the doctrine implicit in medieval theology that men could win their salvation through any merits (good works) of their own. Men were saved, they held, because God willed that they should be saved and not through any ministrations or sacraments of the church. In other words, salvation was given to men because they had faith in God and not because they did good in the world. The major Protestant theologians stressed this view because they felt that the medieval church had placed too much stress on certain practices that suggested that men could buy their way into heaven. In thus arguing, however, leading Protestant thinkers had to face a dilemma. If men were saved by faith alone, then what incentive was there for human beings to live decent, moral lives? This problem Calvin felt he had solved when he argued that those who possessed faith and were truly among the "elect" chosen for salvation could not be immoral. On the contrary, because they were saved, they would "demonstrate their election" by their austerity, self-denial, and personal morality. This theory, some historians have contended, led the Calvinist to an extreme emphasis on individual morality that made him a hard-working, frugal, productive member of society. Because these virtues are conducive to the accumulation of wealth, it has also been argued that Calvanism was a religion peculiarly favorable to the development of modern capitalism. There may be an element of truth to the argument, though it does not take into consideration one or two important facts: first, that such virtues are not always peculiar to Protestant or, specifically, Calvinist societies; and second, that in their social thinking and attitudes the Catholics and Protestants of the sixteenth and seventeenth centuries shared many views.

In somewhat the same way it has been said that Protestantism was largely responsible for modern liberalism and democracy because it promoted religious toleration, emphasized religious individualism, and among some sects used the forms of representative government. Again, such arguments may have some validity if we recognize that these results were quite indirect and inadvertent. At their inception many of the larger Protestant denominations were not believers in religious toleration and, in many cases, came round to it only when it was clear that their own churches were not going to supplant all others. Nor were Protestants, over all, believers in democracy in the sixteenth and seventeenth centuries. Like most other Europeans of the period, they would have been horrified at the modern democratic state.

In one important area, but again indirectly, Protestantism seems to have had a significant effect, though even this one should not be exag-

the poet John Milton, Oliver Cromwell, and the New England theologian John Cotton; the General Baptists, believed to have been founded by the English nonconformist clergyman John Smyth in 1611; and the Quakers, founded by George Fox (1624–1691) about 1647.

gerated. This was the influence of Protestantism on the rise of modern nationalism. Some, but by no means all, of the Protestant churches, and particularly those that, like the Church of England, became state-supported or state-established institutions, tended to unite patriotism and denominationalism by coming under the control of the state. In this way, though it was usually not their intention to do so, they helped to destroy the older, organized unity of Christendom, which had been one of the major characteristics of medieval civilization.

After all, it should not be forgotten that Protestantism, whatever its social or political effects, was still a religious movement concerned with religious aims and purposes. We should be careful not to read backward into it (or other historical movements for that matter) ideas and attitudes that were completely alien to its point of view.

chapter eight

EVENTS AND DEFINITIONS

The historical period between 1500 and 1800 is sometimes called the Age of the Absolute Monarchies, a term that describes the characteristic rule of most European states by hereditary monarchical government largely unchecked by any methods of mass control. After 1800, as a result of changes introduced into the climate of European opinion by the French Revolution, the unchecked form of hereditary monarchy began to be transformed into "constitutional" or "parliamentary" monarchy, in which the ultimate decision-marking power of kings came to be limited by various systems of representative government.

The whole system of international monarchy during these centuries was controlled by a handful of ruling or royal families, whose various branches intermarried so frequently as to create a limited international ruling class. It might have been expected that such an international family system would have preserved the peace and stability of Europe by the need to maintain a common interest. The fact that it did not do so—or did so only in a most limited and temporary way—is an indication of the extent to which the interests of the royal family system tended to be subordinated to the power ambitions of individual rulers. The most important dynastic units of the period between 1500 and 1800 are listed below.

The Age of the Absolute Monarchies

THE ESSENTIAL MOVEMENT

The period from the sixteenth through the eighteenth centuries was a time when most of the nations of modern Europe took the form in which we know them today. In almost every major western country the power of the king had grown to a point where those other elements in society— i.e., the feudal nobility and the church—that had formerly acted as checks on royal authority, were now either completely broken or else absorbed into the royal administration. There were, of course, exceptions to this pattern of development, most notably England, where the power of the crown was drastically curbed by the end of the seventeenth century. But, in the main, the 300 years between 1500 and 1800 saw the monarchs of Europe victorious in the extension of their power and authority. As we have seen, European kings from the Middle Ages onward had come more and more to symbolize the new, impersonal nation-state. The king's law, the civil administration, and the standing army were all instruments of a new kind of statecraft; while these instruments were employed to serve the interests of the king, they were also intended to serve the society over which the crown had absolute power. This was the ideal of absolute monarchy, and in the degree that it approached this ideal it was successful in maintain-

1. ENGLAND (AFTER 1603 KNOWN AS GREAT BRITAIN)

a. The Tudors, 1485–1603. Henry VII, 1485–1509; Henry VIII, 1509–1547; Edward VI, 1547–1553; Mary, 1553–1558; Elizabeth I, 1558–1603.

b. The Stuarts, 1603–1714. James VI (of Scotland) became James I of England, 1603–1625; Charles I, 1625–1649; interregnum (rule of the army leaders, most important of whom was Oliver Cromwell, d. 1658), 1649–1660; Charles II, 1660–1685; James II, 1685–1688; William and Mary, 1688–1702; Anne, 1702–1714.

c. The Hanoverians (House of Brunswick). George I, 1714–1727; George II, 1727–1760; George III, 1760–1820.

2. FRANCE

a. Valois Kings. Charles VIII, 1498–1515; Francis I, 1515–1547; Henry II, 1547–1559; Francis II, 1559–1560; Charles IX, 1560–1574; Henry III, 1574–1589.

b. Bourbon Kings. Henry IV, 1589–1610; Louis XIII, 1610–1643; Louis XIV, 1643–1715; Louis XV, 1715–1774; Louis XVI, 1774–1792.

3. HOLY ROMAN EMPIRE (HOUSE OF HAPSBURG)

Maximilian I, 1493–1519; Charles V, 1519–1556; Ferdinand I, 1556–1564; Maximilian II, 1564–1576; Rudolf II, 1567–1612; Mathias, 1612–1619; Ferdinand II, 1619–1637; Ferdinand III, 1637–1657; Leopold I, 1658–1705; Joseph I, 1705–1711; Charles VI, 1711–1740; Francis I (of Lorraine), 1745–1765, and Maria Theresa, 1740–1780; Joseph II, 1765–1790; Leopold II, 1790–1792; Francis II (took title of Francis I of Austria after 1806), 1792–1835.

4. RUSSIA (ROMANOVS)

Michael, 1613–1645; Alexis, 1645–1676; Theodore III, 1676–1682; Ivan V, 1682–1689; Peter I (the Great), 1689–1725; Catherine I, 1725–1727; Peter II, 1727–1730; Anna, 1730–1740; Elizabeth, 1741–1762; Catherine II (the Great), 1762–1796; Paul I, 1796–1801.

5. PRUSSIA (HOHENZOLLERNS)

Frederick William (the Great Elector), 1640–1688; Frederick I (first Prussian king), 1688–1713; Frederick William I, 1713–1740; Frederick II (the Great), 1740–1786; Frederick William II, 1786–1797; Frederick William III, 1797–1840.

ing itself. Unfortunately, however, this kind of state had several great weaknesses, which in the end wrought its undoing. First, its efficiency and impartiality depended not only upon a bureaucracy (whose members often entrenched themselves in offices that were bought and sold or passed from father to son) but also upon the personal abilities of a sovereign (whose qualities as a ruler, because of the uncertainties of dynastic inheritance, varied greatly from generation to generation). Second, though western European kings were to some extent limited in their absolute freedom to make political decisions, nothing short of rebellion or military defeat by a neighboring state could keep them from carrying out policies that were sometimes dangerous to the welfare of their subjects. And third, while the absolute monarchy did a great deal to destroy the powers and privileges of the nobility, it did not erase them entirely and, in some cases, actually increased them so long as the nobles were willing to become the servants and supporters of the state. These three weaknesses, coupled with rising costs of government from the sixteenth century onward, created a number of complex problems with which absolute governments were less and less able to cope successfully.

A. DYNASTIC CONFLICTS AND WARS OF RELIGION

1. SPAIN

Reign of Ferdinand and Isabella (1479–1516) saw the union of Castile and Aragon, the downfall of the last Moorish state, and the beginning of Spanish overseas expansion. Charles I (of Spain) became king (1516–1556) and Holy Roman Emperor as Charles V, 1519–1556. Hapsburg-Valois rivalry led to wars with France—1521–1529; 1535–1538; 1542–1545; 1551–1559—which ended with the Treaty of Cateau-Cambrésis, a Spanish triumph that marked the high point of Spanish influence in Europe.

Philip II (1556–1598) committed Spain to the cause of the Catholic Reformation: (1) revolt of the Netherlands, 1568–1609; (2) attempt to invade England—defeat of the Spanish Armada, 1588; (3) intervention in French Wars of Religion, 1589–1598.

Spain entered the Thirty Years' War (1618–1648) on the side of the Austrian Hapsburgs against France. Defeat of the Spanish army by French at Rocroi, 1643, marked the end of Spanish military supremacy in Europe. Treaty of the Pyrenees (1659) signaled the decline of Spain and the rise of France.

Reign of Charles II, 1665–1700, last of the Spanish Hapsburgs. To avoid controversy over succession, England, Holland, and France undertook to dispose of Spain and its empire by private agreement, 1698. King Charles, in anger, left his throne to Philip of Anjou, grandson of Louis XIV of France. Austria, England, and Holland formed the Grand Alliance, 1701, to prevent possible union of French and Spanish crowns. War of Spanish Succession, 1701–1714.

2. FRANCE

Reign of Francis I (1515–1547) marked by the so-called Hapsburg-Valois Wars (*see* Spain *above*) and beginning of Protestant movement in France. Treaty of Cateau-Cambrésis (*see* Spain *above*), 1559. Wars of Religion, 1563–1598 (*see* Calvinism, chapter 6). Reign of Henry IV (1589–1610) marked by restoration of strong monarchy and granting of toleration to Huguenots (Edict of Nantes, 1598).

Louis XIII (1610–1643) made Cardinal Richelieu (in power from 1624 to 1642) his chief adviser. The latter (1) broke the independent power of the Huguenots, (2) strengthened the monarchy by checking the feudal nobles, and (3) curbed the House of Hapsburg by intervening in the Thirty Years' War on the side of the German Protestants (1635–1648).

Reign of Louis XIV (1643–1715) saw the emergence of France as the leading power of Europe. Treaty of the Pyrenees, 1659 (*see* Spain *above*). Colbert as controller-general of finances (1662–1683) stimulated French

A. DYNASTIC CONFLICTS AND WARS OF RELIGION

In the period between 1500 and 1715 the territorial and dynastic ambitions of the various European states led to an almost incessant warfare, which gave the ascendancy first to one power or group of powers and then to another. These contests were not simply straightforward struggles for lands and power but were complicated by the religious divisions of the Reformation. Just as there were Catholic and Protestant parties that fought savage civil wars in many countries, so, too, there were Catholic and Protestant nations whose interests divided the whole of Europe into armed camps. In time, however, while religious motives were occasionally strong enough to sway the policies of particular rulers or countries, other more mundane considerations came to have an increasing effect on national policies. By the end of the sixteenth century it was already possible to observe the rather frequent crossing of religious lines in order to form alliances. A generation later, with the coming of the Thirty Years' War, such practices were quite common. Nonetheless, in spite of the decline of religious partisanship as a cause of wars, many conflicts were greatly intensified when religious zeal coincided with other motives. This was one of the major reasons why the wars of the period from 1500 to 1715 were often fought with an unexampled bitterness that did not subside until after the signing of the Peace of Westphalia in 1648.

Let us now look briefly at the role of several of the more important states in the international affairs of this troubled period.

1. SPAIN

The sixteenth century was the era of Spain's greatest power. By the year 1500 a number of smaller kingdoms in the Iberian Peninsula had been consolidated under two rulers, Ferdinand and Isabella. They had destroyed the last vestiges of the ancient Islamic power and embarked on an ambitious program of overseas exploration and colonization, which was destined to bring wealth and greatness to the newly unified Spanish kingdom. Through intermarriage, the crowns of Spain and the Holy Roman Empire came into the possession of a single dynasty (Hapsburgs), whose leading representative, Emperor Charles V, was the most powerful ruler of the sixteenth century. Even so, Charles, a devout Catholic, was not able to check the rise of Lutheranism in Germany. Neither could he entirely eliminate the danger to his family territories arising out of his long rivalry with France. Nevertheless, Charles at his abdication was able to leave to his son, who became Philip II of Spain (1556–1598), a rich inheritance of lands and power.

economic growth and created the system of mercantilism in its classic form (see p. 137). Wars of Devolution, 1667–1668 (over the Spanish Netherlands) and 1672–1678 (against Holland). Revocation of the Edict of Nantes (1685) forced thousands of Huguenots into exile. War of the League of Augsburg (over the Rhenish Palatinate), 1688–1697. War of the Spanish Succession (over uniting the crowns of Spain and France), 1701–1714. Treaties of Utrecht (1713) and Rastadt (1714) provided that Louis XIV's grandson Philip V should remain on the Spanish throne but that France and Spain should never be unified. Death of Louis XIV (1715) left France severely strained in finances and manpower. Louis XV, 1715–1774, great-grandson of Louis XIV, succeeded. "Mississippi Bubble," 1718–1720, caused by speculation promoted by the financier John Law. France participated in the War of the Polish Succession in alliance with Spain and Sardinia, 1733–1738. War of the Austrian Succession, in which France, allied with Prussia, supported the Bavarian elector's claims to the Holy Roman Empire against Maria Theresa, 1740–1748. Diplomatic revolution saw France allied with the Hapsburgs for the first time in history in the ensuing Seven Years' War, 1756–1763.

3. ENGLAND

Reign of Henry VII (1485–1509); order restored after the Wars of the Roses; monarchy strengthened; Court of Star Chamber established, 1487. Reign of Henry VIII (1509–1547) chancellorship of Cardinal Wolsey, 1515–1529; Act of Supremacy made Henry head of the English Church, 1534 (for other changes, see Anglicanism, chapter 6).

Reign of Elizabeth I (1558–1603): defeat of the Spanish Armada, 1588; Golden Age of English literature.

Reign of James I (1603–1625): conflict with Parliament over finances and extension of royal power, 1604–1624.

Reign of Charles I (1625–1649): Petition of Right, 1628; dissolution of parliament and eleven years of personal rule, 1629–1640; Scottish rebellion (1637–1640) forced Charles to call the Long Parliament in 1640; civil wars, 1642–1649; execution of Charles I, 1649.

Commonwealth and Protectorate, 1649–1660: Commonwealth (republic) supplanted the monarchy, 1649–1653; Oliver Cromwell (1599–1658) assumed title of Lord Protector, 1653–1658.

Restoration of the monarchy (1660); reign of Charles II, 1660–1685: Clarendon Code (for the suppression of Protestant dissenters who were not members of the Church of England) formulated, 1661–1665; Charles II and Parliament in conflict over the right of his Catholic brother James to succeed to the throne, 1679–1681; Charles attacked the leaders of the Whig party (which favored religious toleration and limited monarchy) and tried to re-establish absolute rule in England, 1681–1685.

Philip, who was the epitome of the hard-working absolute monarch, at once embarked on a series of projects that were to weaken Spain permanently. All vestiges of religious dissent were ruthlessly suppressed in his dominions. Spanish commerce and industry were rigorously controlled. The military strength of Spain was committed to the cause of the Catholic Reformation and to the weakening of the French monarchy. Philip's most disastrous policies led to a protracted rebellion in the Low Countries, by which Holland finally won its independence, and also to an unsuccessful attempt to conquer England, which failed with the defeat of the Spanish armada by the English in 1588. The last years of Philip's life ended in defeat at the hands of the resurgent French monarchy. From these disasters Spain never recovered, though she was to remain a major force in European politics during the first half of the seventeenth century. By the year 1700 the Spanish kingdom had sunk to the level of a second-rate power.

2. FRANCE

The French monarchy, which through many vicissitudes had declined from a peak of greatness in the thirteenth century to the low point of English conquest during the Hundred Years' War (1338–1453), emerged at the end of the fifteenth century as one of the strong states of Europe. With the accession of Francis I (1515–1547) began the long rivalry between the French kings and the Hapsburgs, which was to influence European international relations for more than two centuries. Despite his incessant wars, Francis strengthened the monarchy and during the period of religious upheaval kept France firmly Catholic, although a large segment of the French population was won over to Calvinism. In the reign of his grandson, Charles IX, a series of civil wars began between Catholics and Huguenots (Protestants), which lasted to the end of the sixteenth century. These were not terminated until the former Protestant prince, Henry IV (1589–1610), issued the Edict of Nantes (1598) granting religious toleration and a measure of security to the Huguenots.

Under Henry and his successors, Louis XIII (1610–1643) and Louis XIV (1643–1715), both the French state and French society underwent a process of reconstruction after the long period of religious struggle. As a consequence, France emerged during the last half of the century as the leading nation of Europe. The architects of this reconstruction were Cardinal Richelieu (1585–1642) under Louis XIII, and Cardinal Mazarin (1602–1661) under Louis XIV. Through their efforts the royal government was made transcendent over French localism and various elements (Huguenots and nobles) potentially dangerous to the

Reign of James II (last Catholic king of England), 1685–1688: James attempted to reestablish the Catholic faith and provoked the Glorious Revolution of 1688.

Reign of Mary II with William III (of Orange), who had been invited to the English throne, 1689–1702: Bill of Rights, 1689, permanently limited royal power; Act of Settlement, 1701, reserved the English throne for Protestants.

Reign of Anne, 1702–1714: union of England with Scotland, 1707; Peace of Utrecht (1713) saw England's emergence as the leading maritime power of Europe.

Reign of George I (formerly ruler of the small German state of Hanover), 1714–1727: beginning of modern cabinet government under Sir Robert Walpole, first prime minister of England, 1721–1742.

George II, 1727–1760), continued Walpole in office. War of Jenkins' Ear with Spain, 1739–1748; England participated in the War of the Austrian Succession from 1744–1748 as an ally of Austria. Second Jacobite Rebellion, known as "The Forty-five," attempted to place the Stuart pretender, Charles Edward ("Bonnie Prince Charlie"), on the British throne; rebels decisively defeated at Culloden, 1745–1746. Seven Years' War between England and France, 1756–1763. Great war ministry of William Pitt the Elder led England to victory, 1757–1761. Reign of George III, 1760–1820. Peace of Paris terminated war, 1763.

Britain, as a result of the Peace of Paris, created what is known as the "first British Empire," a vast collection of territories stretching around the globe from North America to India. British influence in India was unchallenged by any other European power after 1763. Canada was transferred from French to British control at Peace of Paris, 1763.

During the course of the eighteenth century a combination of economic and social causes began the major transformation, clearly manifest after 1775, that is known as the Industrial Revolution. The major effects of this great breakthrough on the productive processes of British society did not begin to be felt decisively until after 1790.

War of the American Revolution, 1775–1783, found Britain isolated and forced to face a strong coalition of European powers (France, Holland, Spain) that supported the rebellion of the British colonies in North America against the mother country. Independence of United States recognized by Treaty of Paris, 1783, which ended the period of the first British Empire.

4. THE HOLY ROMAN EMPIRE

Reign of Charles V (1519–1556). Abdication of Charles, 1556, permanently separated Spain and the empire under two separated branches of the Hapsburg family.

state were deprived of any further power to do harm. Nevertheless, the state did its best to strengthen the economy through the protection of French manufactures and the strict regulation of foreign trade. This policy, known as mercantilism, was fully developed and put into practice by Colbert (1619–1683), the finance minister of Louis XIV. The work of these three men enabled King Louis to embark on the series of expansionist wars at the end of the sevententh century that, while they made France feared throughout Europe, disastrously weakened the internal structure of French society and dissipated its laboriously accumulated wealth.

In spite of the unfortunate foreign policy of Louis, the late seventeenth century was one of the brilliant periods of French history. Cultivated persons everywhere looked to France for cultural inspiration, and the French language became a second tongue for the social and intellectual elites of Europe. This, too, was a great era of French literature which produced such names as Corneille (1606–1684), Molière (1622–1673), and Racine (1639–1699).

3. ENGLAND

The history of the English monarchy during the sixteenth and seventeenth centuries was, in its conclusion, quite different from that of France or Spain. For more than 150 years, however—from 1485 to 1640—it looked as though England, too, would go the way of most other western European states and become permanently an absolute monarchy. Under the strong Tudor dynasty, whose leading representatives were Henry VII (1485–1509), Henry VIII (1509–1547), and Elizabeth I (1558–1603), every tendency pointed in that direction. By reducing the English nobility to obedience, assuming the headship of the church, and reorganizing the machinery of government, these monarchs gave to England a state with all the characteristics of the new kind of monarchy. Though less popular and less able than their Tudor successors, the first two kings of the house of Stuart, James I (1603–1625) and Charles I (1625–1649), tried to carry on with these developments; however, they met disaster in the attempt. In the middle of the seventeenth century the growth of royal absolutism was suddenly checked by the outbreak of civil war. After a long period of intermittent struggle, which saw the monarchy temporarily replaced by a military dictatorship under Oliver Cromwell (1649–1658), the power of the crown was conclusively curbed by the "Glorious Revolution" of 1688.

Though there are many reasons for England's divergence from the general European pattern of political development, one of the most important was the result of a peculiarly English historical happen-

a. The Thirty Years' War, 1618–1648.   Growing religious rivalry within the empire (among Catholics, Lutherans, and Calvinists) led to Thirty Years' War, which passed through four major phases: (1) the Bohemian period, 1618–1625, when the Bohemians—who had rejected Emperor Ferdinand II as their ruler and elected Frederick V, a Calvinist and elector of the Rhenish Palatinate, as their king—were defeated by the imperial armies; (2) the Danish period, 1625–1629, when Christian IV of Denmark intervened in the war and was forced to withdraw after defeats by the imperial armies; (3) the Swedish period, 1630–1635, when the Swedish king, Gustavus Adolphus, invaded Germany and was everywhere victorious over the imperialists until his death at the Battle of Lützen in 1632; (4) the Swedish-French period, 1635–1648, when Sweden and France in alliance carried on the war against the Holy Roman Emperor.

b. Peace of Westphalia, 1648.   After long war that resulted in serious losses of men and wealth throughout Germany, both sides finally negotiated the Peace of Westphalia, 1648. By its terms the power of the Holy Roman Emperor was reduced to a shadow; religious toleration was won by the Calvinists; and the independence of the Netherlands was recognized. War left German lands in a state of chaos for almost a generation. Slow recovery of the empire: imperial forces drove Turks from Hungary, 1682–1699, but not before the Turks' last siege of Vienna, 1683.

Death of the last male heir of the Hapsburg line (Charles VI, 1711–1740), who had tried to secure the rights of his daughter, Maria Theresa (1740–1780), to the Austrian throne by means of the Pragmatic Sanction, led to the War of the Austrian Succession, 1740–1748.

Diplomatic revolution ended the long rivalry between France and Austria and brought them into alliance against Prussia and England during the Seven Years' War, 1756–1763.

Reign of Joseph II (1765–1790) marked the era of enlightened despotism in Austria.

5. HOLLAND AND SWEDEN

a. Holland.   War of Dutch Independence (two phases: 1568–1609 and 1621–1648) resulted in recognition of Holland's independence at Peace of Westphalia, 1648: duke of Alva sent by Spain to suppress Dutch revolt, 1567; declaration of Dutch independence, 1581; death of William the Silent (prince of Orange), 1584; beginning of Dutch mercantile expansion and overseas settlement, ca. 1595; twelve years' truce between Dutch and Spaniards, 1609–1621; renewal of hostilities, 1621–1648, ended in formal recognition of Dutch freedom.

First Anglo-Dutch War, 1652–1654, resulted directly from passage of

stance. England, unlike the continental states, had not only preserved its medieval representative body, the parliament, but had seen that body grow in strength until it had become an integral part of the English system of government. Theoretically, even so late as the seventeenth century, Parliament was not an independent political body representing the will of the people but a dependent institution, which the king might merely consult in public matters and which he did not have to call into existence at all if he did not wish to. Because the problem of government finance had become serious by the seventeenth century, the king was forced to resort to Parliament more and more often for financial aid. This aid Parliament would give him only at the price of his surrendering some of his powers. When in the end Charles I, in desperation, tried to rule entirely without Parliament, this expedient helped to bring on civil war; for Charles, in so doing, challenged a number of discontented groups who were strongly represented in Parliament. These were the country gentlemen (gentry), lawyers, merchants, and the various religious groups who were called Puritans. These groups spearheaded the opposition to the crown and, throughout the century, continually tried to hold its power in check.

With the Glorious Revolution of 1688, England did not become at once either a democracy or a constitutional monarchy in the modern sense. Rather it became a state in which the final constitutional power was controlled by a rather limited elite of landholding nobles and gentlemen and a few wealthy merchants who were strong enough to make their influence felt in Parliament. Though the English electoral system was to remain thoroughly unrepresentative until it was drastically reformed in the nineteenth century, the revolution engineered by this small aristocratic oligarchy of Englishmen in 1688 was not without great historical significance. Not only did it become the model that justified later revolutions, including those in America and France, but it helped to preserve the traditions of parliamentary government at a moment when they were rapidly disappearing in other parts of Europe.

In other ways, too, the history of England during the sixteenth and seventeenth centuries was marked by developments of importance to the Western World. This was a remarkable era of English intellectual and social vitality, which had its beginnings in one of the great periods of the world's history, the "Golden Age" of Queen Elizabeth. English seamen, such as Drake and Hawkins, pushed into seas previously unknown to England and destroyed the seapower of Spain with their daring. A generation after the defeat of the Spanish armada in 1588 the first English settlements were made in North America. With these events the whole of the Western Hemisphere came under Euro-

English Navigation Act (1651), which restricted English trade to English shipping, and from Anglo-Dutch rivalry in the Far East. Second Anglo-Dutch War, 1665–1667, resulted in exchange of New Amsterdam (New York) for Surinam. Triple Alliance (England, Holland, and Sweden) formed, 1668, to curb ambitions of Louis XIV of France. Despite the alliance, Third Anglo-Dutch War ensued, 1672–1678. William III (of Orange), Dutch statesman, and Mary, his wife, invited to English throne as a result of Revolution of 1688.

b.   Sweden.   Gustavus I (Vasa) led successful rebellion against Denmark, 1520, and became king, 1523–1560; beginning of Swedish expansion into Baltic region. Sweden accepted Lutheranism, 1527, Eric XIV, 1560–1568, continued expansion of Swedish power in Baltic area. Gustavus Adolphus, 1611–1632, made Sweden the leading Baltic power; intervened successfully in Thirty Years' War (see Holy Roman Empire above). Reign of Charles XII, 1697–1718, marked the decline of Swedish power: Swedes defeated by Russians at Poltava, 1709; treaty of Nystadt, 1721, ended Sweden's dominance of the Baltic.

Hostilities with Russia renewed by Sweden in an effort to regain lost territories, 1741–1743. By terms of the Treaty Abö (1743) Sweden was forced to cede Finland to the Russians. Third Russian war, 1788–1790, achieved initial successes; Swedes finally forced to conclude the Treaty of Wereloe which left Russia in possession of Finland and Karelia.

pean colonization and was thus destined to become a part of the larger community of Western Civilization. In literature, Shakespeare (1564–1616), Spenser (ca. 1552–1599), and Milton (1608–1674) stand out amid a cluster of others who helped to make this one of the major epochs in the history of English writing, for each of these was to have an influence reaching far beyond his native land.

4. THE HOLY ROMAN EMPIRE

By 1500 the Holy Roman Empire, which was originally intended to be the proud successor of the first Roman Empire, had become a loose confederation made up largely of small German-speaking principalities that acknowledged the rule of the Hapsburgs as nominally elected emperors. Unlike France or England, the empire had never developed a centralized government, and the rise of Lutheranism and Calvinism furthered its disunity by dividing the Catholic emperors from their large body of Protestant subjects. In the first quarter of the seventeenth century tension between the two camps finally led to the outbreak of a long and unhappy war. This struggle, known as the Thirty Years' War (1618–1648), was more than just a religious conflict. At stake also was the question of imperial authority. If the emperor could make himself master of a strong, unified empire whose princes were dependent directly upon his rule, then the old Holy Roman Empire might well become the most powerful state in Europe. It was in fear of this eventuality, as well as for religious reasons, that other European states came to be involved in the struggle. Before it was finished, at one time or another England, the Netherlands, Denmark, Spain, Sweden (under its great king, Gustavus Adolphus), and France had all taken part on one or the other side in the conflict. The war had three significant results in that at its conclusion (Peace of Westphalia, 1648), the hope of uniting all German-speaking lands under a single ruler was virtually ended until the nineteenth century, Spain was further weakened as a major European power, and France had emerged as the strongest continental state.

During the late seventeenth century the Hapsburg lands of the Holy Roman Empire, whose core was the modern state of Austria, slowly recovered from the effects of the Thirty Years' War, although a major crisis occurred in 1683 when a Turkish army very nearly captured Vienna. The city was saved by a relief force led by the Polish monarch John Sobieski (1674–1696). For the next two generations the resurgent Hapsburg monarchy undertook a European counteroffensive against the Turks, which did not end until Turkey had ceased to be a significant European power.

B. THE SHIFT TO EASTERN EUROPE: PRUSSIA AND RUSSIA

1. PRUSSIA (BRANDENBURG)

Union of Prussia and the electorate of Brandenburg by inheritance, 1618. Reign of Frederick William the Great Elector, 1640–1688, saw the building of a strong army and a centralized government. Frederick III, elector of Brandenburg, assumed title of king in Prussia, 1701. Frederick William I (1713–1740) created powerful Prussian army. Frederick II (the Great), 1740–1786, conquered Silesia in the War of the Austrian Succession, 1740–1748, and in alliance with England against Austria, France, and Russia successfully fought to keep it during the Seven Years' War, 1756–1763. Prussia remained one of the leading military powers of Europe until the Napoleonic era.

Nevertheless, dynastic difficulties raised the question of royal succession on the death of the last male Hapsburg heir, Emperor Charles VI, in 1740. The subsequent War of the Austrian Succession, 1740–1748, left the Hapsburg dominions in a state of permanent national weakness, despite the efforts of Emperor Joseph II (1765–1790; see p. 164) to introduce reforms intended to transform the monarchy into an "enlightened" modern state. During the following 130 years until 1918 the Hapsburg monarchy survived as the Austrian Empire, which after 1867 was called Austria-Hungary. The Holy Roman Empire disappeared in 1806 when Francis II resigned the title of Holy Roman Emperor to become Emperor Francis I (1804–1835) of Austria.

5. HOLLAND AND SWEDEN

The seventeenth century also saw the rise of two lesser states, Holland and Sweden, to brief periods of greatness. After 1600 Holland, following a long struggle against Spain for her independence, became one of the leading colonial powers of Europe. By developing her seapower and commercial skills, this small country was able to play the role of a great state until the beginning of the seventeenth century, despite a relatively small population and a scarcity of natural resources. Sweden, on the other hand, while even poorer in resources and population, had the advantage of able leadership and excellent military organization, which made it possible for the Swedes to dominate the Baltic regions and parts of northern Europe throughout the seventeenth century. With the rise of Russia after 1700, Sweden's position rapidly declined to that of a lesser European state.

B. THE SHIFT TO EASTERN EUROPE: PRUSSIA AND RUSSIA

Until the end of the seventeenth century the focus of European events was upon the long-established states and kingdoms of western Europe. After 1700 this focus was broadened to include two new states, Prussia and Russia, whose emergence as major powers was to alter permanently the old system of international relationships in Europe. Both of these new monarchies came into existence at a time when absolutism was at its height in the West. Therefore, they were able to incorporate into their systems of government all the institutions and practices of the new absolutism without at the same time accepting the long-established forms of law and the customary sanctions that tended to limit the powers of western absolute monarchs. As a consequence, the sovereigns of

Treaty of Hubertusburg, 1763, guaranteed Prussia's retention of the conquered territory of Silesia. Series of domestic measures undertaken by Frederick II intended to restore Prussia after the war: remission of provincial taxes; establishment of central bank at Berlin (1765); major drainage projects. For all of these efforts, Prussia remained a not very happy model of eighteenth-century autocracy.

2. RUSSIA

Reign of Ivan III (the Great), 1462–1505, first Russian national ruler. Ivan IV (1533–1584) formally assumed title of tsar (czar) and thus laid claim to the pretensions of the Byzantine emperors. Russian patriarchate separate from that of Constantinople established, 1589.

Civil war ("time of troubles") resulted in the calling of the Romanov dynasty to the Russian throne, 1613.

Peter I (the Great), 1689–1725, undertook to "westernize" Russia and to transform it into a significant European power. His aims: (1) to give Russia an outlet to the sea; (2) to make the country strong militarily and economically by introducing western European skills; and (3) to increase the central authority of the state over church and nobles. In the Great Northern War, 1700–1721, Peter broke Sweden's power in the north; though first defeated by Charles XII at Narva, 1700, Peter later won a decisive victory over the Swedes at Poltava, 1709. Peter's internal reforms: nobility made to serve the state; industry and trade encouraged; government of the Orthodox church brought under control of the state. Treaty of Nystadt, 1721, marked Russia's emergence as the leading northern power. Russia emerged as a major European military power by participating in the Seven Years' War, 1756–1763, in alliance with Austria and France against Frederick the Great. First Russian university founded in Moscow, 1755. Reign of Catherine the Great, 1762–1796, saw an extension of Peter the Great's work of reform; Russian expansion in Turkey and Siberia began; ancient kingdom of Poland partitioned among Russia, Austria, and Prussia in 1772, 1793, and 1795.

Prussia and Russia were able to construct state systems that were far more efficient in the exercise of power, far more authoritarian, and, in some ways, far more ruthless than any existing in western Europe.

1. PRUSSIA

With little exaggeration, it is possible to say that the kingdom of Prussia was created by a continuous and deliberate act of will on the part of an able line of north German princes whose reigns extended over a period of about 150 years (1640–1786). The territory from which these Hohenzollern rulers first began to expand their power consisted of the old border, or march (mark), lands of Brandenburg in north central Germany, an area neither particularly fertile nor unusually endowed with natural resources. By clever manipulation and remarkable foresight the rulers of Brandenburg (known as "electoral princes" in the seventeenth century and as "kings of Prussia" after 1701) were able to outmaneuver their neighbors diplomatically and to build up their civil service and army with such effect that by the opening of the eighteenth century their small state of Prussia had expanded into a formidable European power. With the accession of Frederick the Great (1740–1786), the new kingdom possessed a leader of genius and daring who led his country in successful wars with its far more powerful neighbors and, at one period during the Seven Years' War (1756–1763), actually kept at bay a powerful alliance of Austria, France, and Russia. The great effort required for so small a country to maintain itself as a major power forced the Prussian state to subordinate other forms of social activity to the interests of military establishment and led to the founding of a military caste and a tradition as harsh and demanding in its ways as that of Sparta in the ancient world.

2. RUSSIA

Of equal significance to Western civilization was the emergence of Russia as a European power during the same period. For centuries, the Slavic peoples of the great eastern European plain had been isolated from the mainstream of western European development. During the early Middle Ages Latin Christian missionaries had converted the Poles (ca. 963) and brought the medieval kingdom of Poland into western Christendom. At about the same time, German colonists, pushing eastward across the Elbe and Oder rivers, had conquered and Christianized other groups of Slavs. Both movements had stopped short of the area now known as Russia, which as a consequence came under influences and developed a society and customs somewhat different from those of the western European community of states. The missionary efforts

C. THE WORLD OF EIGHTEENTH-CENTURY EUROPE

The seventeenth century witnessed a less spectacular but more consistent expansion of European holdings overseas. Although there were few major discoveries, colonization and development went on apace, so that by the end of the century the worldwide commercial network created by the European imperial system had virtually come into being. In general, European colonization tended to follow three patterns: (1) In regions like Latin America a resident aristocracy of Spaniards and Portuguese ruled a large and long-settled but relatively primitive population who worked for the ruling Europeans as a labor force; to some extent the Europeans intermarried with the native population. (2) Elsewhere, in North America for example, where the native population was too sparse to furnish an adequate labor force, Europeans pushed the natives aside and established European communities whose inhabitants lived by their own labors and in so doing made use of European skills and techniques. (3) In most parts of Africa and Asia the Europeans did not settle in great numbers but sought only to establish trading stations and to develop commercial monopolies.

Only in the Far East did the ancient Asian states of China and Japan preserve themselves against the flood of European power during the eighteenth century. For these societies, however, the impact of the West

of the Greek Orthodox church brought Russian lands within the Greek Christian orbit; then a period of Tartar rule, beginning in the thirteenth century, kept the peoples of the area in isolation from the West. Not until the fifteenth century did the modern state begin to expand outward from the principality of Muscovy (Moscow). As it grew, its rulers began to think of themselves as the Caesars (czars or tsars) of the "third Rome" and took on the style and manner of Byzantine autocrats, while their power was greatly enhanced by the unsettled conditions of the Russian frontiers. By the seventeenth century the Russian state was pressing hard against the older Slavic kingdoms of Poland and Lithuania as it gradually moved its borders westward.

At this juncture there came to the Russian throne the famous "westernizing" tsar, Peter the Great (1689–1725), who deliberately initiated a policy intended to bring Russia up to the western level of military and economic strength. With ruthless energy he made his country a European power for the first time in its history. Though it was for long inferior to the rest of Europe in its economic and technical development, the appearance of such a vast sprawling state with expansionist tendencies was to change the European balance of power permanently.

C. THE WORLD OF EIGHTEENTH-CENTURY EUROPE

By the opening of the eighteenth century a significant change had taken place in the relations of western Europe with the rest of the world. While Europe's wars were still fought over European objectives—that is, territorial rivalries, dynastic ambitions, and power alignments—a new and important element began to play an often decisive part in the diplomatic and military strategy of European states. Heretofore, struggles over colonies or commercial concessions in other parts of the world had been localized affairs that did not always affect the welfare or the position of a particular state in international politics. After 1700, however, victory or defeat in remote areas like India or North America sometimes determined the outcome of the European war.

The reason for this change is not far to seek. A significant part of Europe's economic well-being now depended upon overseas connections. Great amounts of capital and large numbers of Europeans had migrated to lands outside Europe. Indirectly, of course, the economic power of the new relationship had been making itself felt in Europe for generations. Since the sixteenth century the gold and silver brought to Spain from the New World had been pumped, in the regular course of commercial exchange, into the European economic system. As a result,

brought about a painful transition, for in their different ways both China and Japan sought to fend off western influences either by ignoring them (in the case of China) or by retiring into social and geographic isolation (in the case of Japan). In neither instance were they permitted to do so, although Japan was more fortunate in keeping control over its destinies from the late nineteenth century onward. The imperial Chinese state and society, weakened by the pressure of massive population increase and burdened by a technology that could no longer serve its subsistence needs, succumbed during the nineteenth century to western infiltration and coercion.

D. THE EIGHTEENTH-CENTURY STRUGGLE FOR OVERSEAS EMPIRE

In the Peace of Utrecht (1713; War of the Spanish Succession) Britain gained from France, Acadia, Hudson's Bay, Newfoundland, and St. Kitts; from Spain, Gibraltar and the right to trade with Spanish colonies for thirty years (the *Asiento*).

The Treaty of Aix-la-Chapelle (1748; War of Austrian Succession) provided for the mutual restoration of colonial conquests.

In the Treaty of Paris (1763; Seven Years' War) Britain gained from France, Canada and Cape Breton Island, Grenada in the West Indies, and French possessions on the Senegal in Africa; from Spain, Florida. Britain restored Goree in Africa and Pondichery and Chandernagor in India to France; Cuba was returned by Britain to Spain. This treaty marked the height of Britain's colonial power in the eighteenth century.

In the Treaty of Paris (1783; War of the American Revolution) Britain granted independence to American colonies, Tobago and Senegal to France, Minorca and Florida to Spain. This was the only colonial war of the century in which Britain lost more than she gained.

E. THE SECULARIZATION OF THE MODERN WORLD,
1687 TO THE PRESENT

One of the important transformations in western thought had its beginnings in the late seventeenth century when the shift in outlook called secularization began to take place. What is usually meant by "secularization" is the practice by which men in their beliefs and daily actions seek for explanations of cause and effect in terms of natural phenomena and not in the acts and intentions of divine providence. It was, in short, a tendency to see in every occurrence not the hand of God but an exemplification of laws that could be understood only in "scientific" or "natural" terms. The words

the decline in the purchasing power of money, which had been observable in European life from the fifteenth century onward, became more marked; indeed, it was a "price revolution" that enormously increased the cost of living. The far-reaching effects of this sudden increase contributed to the economic hardship not only of individuals but even governments. The financial difficulties of many European monarchs during the sixteenth and seventeenth centuries, which in turn caused political tensions and upheavals, are indirectly traceable to this economic revolution. In this sense, the European economy was already global, and Europe itself was the center of a complex network of relationships reaching outward to all parts of the earth.

D. THE EIGHTEENTH-CENTURY STRUGGLE FOR OVERSEAS EMPIRE

Two nations, England and France, were more directly involved in and affected by this transformation during the eighteenth century than any others. Holland and Spain both had passed the zenith of their power and no other continental states were in a position to challenge Anglo-French hegemony outside Europe. As a consequence, these two were the major antagonists in a long series of intermittent struggles for empire that lasted for almost a century and terminated on the eve of the French Revolution. In each of these conflicts—the War of the Spanish Succession (1702–1713), the War of the Austrian Succession (1740–1748), the Seven Years' War (1756–1763), and the War of the American Revolution (1778–1783)—England was almost regularly victorious. Only in the War of the American Revolution did she suffer any reversal. It was during this century that England acquired vast territories, which historians have come to call the First British Empire, since a great deal of it, including the colonies in North America, was lost in 1783. England did, however, come into possession of Canada and retain it, and she cemented her hold upon large parts of the subcontinent of India.

of the eighteenth-century philosopher David Hume sum it up for all the generations since: "No new fact can ever be inferred from the religious hypothesis [i.e., the assumption that God exists and controls the universe purposefully]; no event foreseen or foretold; no reward or punishment expected or dreaded beyond what is already known by practice and observation."

The consequences of this shift from the providential to the secular view of history have been profound and reach into every area of western life so significantly that we cannot possibly enumerate all of them. In one area, however, the effect has been so obvious and far-reaching that it may be thought of as one of the major characteristics of the modern world, for good or ill. That effect, of course, is the decline of mass religious faith, combining a steady diminution in the influence of organized religious belief and a decrease in the relative number of religious believers throughout the Western world during the past 250 years. Increasingly, men have thought and lived within the context of this world as opposed to the world of immortality that, according to centuries-old religious belief, awaits those who have attained a proper state of grace and for whom this life is simply a brief preparation. With time, most men came to believe that this life is not necessarily a preparation for eternity but the only period of conscious existence that man will ever know. Perhaps the whole of this secular attitude is best summed up in the popular saying "You only live once."

What this shift in expectation has meant to modern man is difficult to exaggerate, for the whole of his sense of morality, his view of the universe, and his belief in historical purposefulness have been altered by it. In a number of ways, however, he almost unconsciously has preserved certain of the hypotheses about morality, the cosmic order, and historical purpose that he originally derived from Judaism and Christianity. He still believes, for example, that "good" and "bad" things happen, even though his ethical sense is often completely divorced from any faith in the existence of divine authority.

chapter nine

EVENTS AND DEFINITIONS

The Scientific
Revolution and the
Age of Enlightenment

THE ESSENTIAL MOVEMENT

During few periods of his history has western man ever really possessed the confidence to believe that by his reasoning alone he could
fathom all the questions about himself and his existence. For the greater
part of his historic life man has sensed that something unknown or
mysterious lies just beyond his powers of rational explanation. Traditionally, he has assigned that unknown to the sphere of religious faith,
confessing that the universe in all of its mystery is truly explicable
only in terms of the divine. On a few historic occasions, however, the
elation of a great and significant intellectual discovery, which seems to
push the boundaries of his understanding deep into the unknown, has
raised his confidence in his own powers to a point where he believes
himself capable, after all, of finally answering the questions that have
puzzled him since the beginning of time. One period when men came
close to achieving this confidence was during the age of Greek intellectual greatness in the fifth and fourth centuries B.C. Another began
with the opening of the eighteenth century, reached its zenith a few
decades later, and carried over, at least in the sphere of scientific
thought, into the nineteenth and twentieth centuries. Much of this

A. THE SCIENTIFIC REVOLUTION

Many of the earliest and most significant scientific discoveries of the early modern period were made in the field of astronomy. Some of the more important of these were (1) the formulation of the heliocentric (sun-centered) theory of the solar system by Copernicus (1473–1543) whose *On the Revolution of Celestial Bodies* transformed the bases of scientific thought; (2) Johannes Kepler (1571–1630) formulated his three laws of planetary motion; (3) Galileo Galilei (1564–1642) perfected the telescope (1609), which proved the Copernican theory; Galileo also formulated the laws of "local motion" (mechanics); (4) Isaac Newton (1642–1727) published his conclusions on the laws of celestial mechanics (theory of gravitation) in *Principia mathematica* (1687); Pierre Simon de Laplace (1749–1827) completed and developed the Newtonian astronomy in his *Systeme du Monde* (1796).

1. MATHEMATICS AND NATURAL PHILOSOPHY

Francis Bacon (1561–1626) set forth his inductive method and prepared the way for modern experimental method in his *Novum Organum*; René Descartes (1596–1650) wrote *Discourse on Method* and first applied algebraic method to geometry; Blaise Pascal (1632–1662) discovered mathematical theory of probability; Newton and G. W. Leibniz (1646–1716), the German philosopher, independently discovered calculus; Joseph Lagrange (1736–1813) created the calculus of variations and systematized differential equations.

2. MEDICINE, BIOLOGY, AND CHEMISTRY

Theophrastus von Hohenheim (Paracelsus), ca. 1490–1541, broke with the medical tradition of Galen and used chemical drugs in medical practice; Andreas Versalius, 1515–1564, published his great work on anatomy, *Fabrica Humani Corporis* in 1543; William Harvey, 1578–1657, formulated a general theory of blood circulation in his *On the Motion of the Heart* (1628); Anton van Leeuwenhoek, 1632–1723, Dutch microscopist, did not invent the microscope but he did perfect the technique of microscopic observation in scientific experiments; John Ray, 1627–1705, laid the foundations of modern descriptive and systematic biology; Carl Linnaeus (von Linne), 1707–1778, evolved the first successful system of biological classification (1735); Georges Cuvier, 1769–1832, founded the modern science of

confidence remains with us, though doubting voices have been raised in our own time to question, once again, the possibility of man's ultimately knowing all that there is to know about himself and his universe.

A. THE SCIENTIFIC REVOLUTION

What gave the eighteenth century its confidence in the power of man's reason to reduce the unknown was a revolution in thought that had occurred in the century preceding. The seventeenth century was a "century of genius," in the words of the great modern scientific philosopher Alfred North Whitehead, a time when a whole galaxy of outstanding figures suddenly appeared on the intellectual horizon of Europe. Why men like Galileo, Descartes, Newton, and Leibniz were born within the brief span of a single century is something no one can explain. In part, their scientific achievements may have been the result of accident. More probably they were the result of a combination of complex social factors that came together at a particular moment and produced the intellectual stimuli needed for such discoveries.

Another part of the explanation must surely lie in the fact that certain underlying ideas or assumptions, many of them reaching back to the Greeks, were shared by all who speculated in the natural sciences. The most important of these ideas was the assumption that the universe was an ordered and orderly system so regulated that it could be understood by those who had the knowledge, the patience, and the intelligence to do so. The assumption of order in nature was the basis of philosophy and mathematics and had, for centuries, been implicit in the belief that the universe was controlled by fixed and certain natural laws. This faith, however much it may have been modified during the period between the fall of Rome and the High Middle Ages, had never been entirely lost and was, as we have seen, an important part of the intellectual heritage of the medieval philosophers.

The major difficulty with the assumption that the universe was rational and orderly, lay in the fact that much of what men were able to observe empirically—i.e., through their senses—did not always seem to square with the harmony expressed in mathematics and natural law. Fortunately for modern science, thinkers of the later Middle Ages and the Renaissance were not daunted by this apparent contradiction, which made it seem, for example, that the sun traveled round the earth. As the science of mathematics continued to develop, men continued to make use of it to test, to probe, and to explain all the seemingly disordered phenomena of the world in which they lived. In

paleontology; Johann van Helmont, ca. 1580–1644, first studied chemical gases; Robert Boyle, 1627–1691, sought to make clear the fundamental nature of chemical transformation in his *Sceptical Chymist* (1661); Joseph Priestley, 1733–1804, isolated oxygen; Antoine Lavoisier, 1743–1794, proved that while matter may alter its state as a result of chemical reactions, it does not alter its amount.

3. SCIENTIFIC ACADEMIES

One of the ways in which scientific knowledge was accumulated and spread was through the organization of learned bodies or academies. Among the more famous of these were: Accademia Secretorum Naturae (Naples), 1560; Accademia dei Lincei, of which Galileo was a member (Rome), 1603–1630; Royal Society of London, 1662; Académie des Sciences (Paris), 1666.

A more important result of the increasingly large number of persons engaged on various aspects of the scientific enterprise and the appearance of the numerous scientific bodies of the seventeenth and eighteenth centuries was a greater institutionalization of scientific knowledge that manifest itself, for example, in the curricula of the universities and secondary schools. Thus science ceased to be the learned hobby of a few isolated persons and became instead a massive, cumulative undertaking whose recorded knowledge was preserved for posterity.

This institutionalization of scientific knowledge was a matter of the highest importance, for it led to what is sometimes referred to as the "information explosion" of the modern world. Scientists and other scholars found themselves in possession of an evergrowing body of knowledge, which enabled man to expand as never before his awareness of himself and his cosmic surroundings. Furthermore, the diffusion and spread of such information systems in the form of libraries, archives, learned publications, etc., meant that for the first time in human history it was impossible to break the continuity of human knowledge by natural disaster, barbarian conquest, or other disruptive phenomena. Man at long last had minimized the possibility of a sudden recurrence of another dark age in history.

B. THE ENLIGHTENMENT

The Newtonian discoveries appeared to reinforce a method of inquiry, first put forward by Descartes (1596–1650), that seemed to promise great possibilities for the study of man and human society. By searching every field of knowledge for basic axioms whose truth could not be doubted when subjected to the most searching analyses, men might hope to erect a "social science" as accurate and valid as the physical sciences. John Locke

so doing, they sometimes ran foul of the theories of Aristotle, on which a part of medieval theology was based, and thus came into conflict with ecclesiastical authority. Despite these difficulties, their own intellectual aspirations drove them to continue their efforts until a major breakthrough had been achieved in the field of astronomy, where many of the great advances in early modern science were made. The man responsible for this discovery was Nicholas Copernicus (1473–1543), who found that by assuming the sun rather than the earth to be the center of the system of planets, he could explain the movements of the sun, moon, stars, earth, and planets much more clearly, and in simpler mathematical terms. It is important to remember here that Copernicus did not have empirical evidence for the heliocentric (sun-centered) theory when he offered it in place of the geocentric (earth-centered) theory. For the evidence of the senses indicated to him, as it had to men for centuries, that the sun went around the earth. Copernicus proposed the new hypothesis out of a belief that nature was orderly and that this orderliness was compatible with the simpler mathematical expression that the new theory permitted.

With this discovery, the whole science of mathematics, and with it astronomy, underwent a revolution that had far-reaching effects. Within 150 years the search for ever more precise mathematical expressions of natural law had led to the formulation of the laws of mechanics by Galileo and finally to the crowning achievement of the whole scientific revolution, the famous hypothesis of Sir Isaac Newton by which the relations of all bodies in the universe are explained according to three basic laws. The appearance of Newton's *Principles of Mathematics* in 1687 was the signal for a major change in the intellectual climate of Western civilization, for by that time each of the great discoveries had been verified seemingly beyond question with the invention of new measuring devices and new methods of observation. The result seemed to foretell a marvelous future for the human race, which at last appeared to possess a means of plumbing all knowledge.

B. THE ENLIGHTENMENT: THE INTELLECTUAL IMPACT OF THE SCIENTIFIC REVOLUTION

Newton's discoveries had the effect of transforming the thinking of large numbers of Europeans, and the new thinking exalted every form of scientific knowledge. Science accordingly has grown in prestige until it has come to be looked upon by many persons in the Western world as the most important of all intellectual activities. But Newton's dis-

(1632–1704), English philosopher and political theorist, provided the basis for the later philosophies of the Enlightenment in his *Essay Concerning Human Understanding* (1690). Locke declared that he would "inquire into the original, certainty, and extent of human knowledge." His purpose, though seemingly at odds with the methods of Descartes, was really to preserve Cartesian rationalism. Locke believed that all knowledge derived from the senses, that the mind of man was a blank slate (*tabula rasa)*, which is gradually filled with sensory information drawn from experience. In short, though his writings later were seen to have opened the way for an empirical attack on rationalism, Locke really wanted a "middle way" that would comprehend both rationalism and empiricism. In the two generations after Locke his empirical suggestions were carried to a conclusion by two other British "empirical" philosophers: (1) Bishop George Berkeley, 1685–1753, taught in his *Theory of Vision* (1709) that "all that we see is our sensation" and in his *Principles of Human Knowledge*, 1710, that "all that exists is our knowledge." Matter, as Berkeley saw it, had no existence independent of human perception. (2) David Hume, 1711–1776, carried empiricism to its extreme conclusion in his *Treatise on Human Nature* (1739) and thus prepared the way for the philosophical reconstruction of Immanuel Kant and the Romantic School of philosophers.

1. RELIGION

Voltaire (1694–1778) spread the ideas of the English deists in his *Letters on the English* (1734) and his *Elements of the Philosophy of Newton* (1738). David Hume (1711–1776), the Scottish philosopher, expressed religious skepticism in his *Dialogues Concerning Natural Religion* (1779). The leading materialist (atheist) work was Baron Holbach's *System of Nature* (1770), which described the universe as a place where no divine authority exists.

Growth of Deism or "natural religion": Deism, which was most widely accepted in England, was represented by the following: Anthony Collins, 1676–1729, first put forward the Deist position in his *Discourse on Free Thinking* (1713). Matthew Tindal, 1653–1733, author of the most comprehensive treatise on Deism, *Christianity as Old as the Creation* (1730), sometimes called the "Bible of Deism." William Wollaston, 1659–1724, argued in favor of the adequacy of "a religion of reason" to serve men's needs in his *The Religion of Nature Delineated* (1722).

As the century advanced, however, there was a strong reaction among many religious groups to both Deism and rationalism. Among the more important of these groups were John Wesley, 1703–1791, and his followers, later (1784) known as Methodists, who preached salvation through faith

coveries also had an immediate effect that has not proved wholly good, since they convinced many persons that all the complexities of the universe, including the diverse and seemingly unpredictable vagaries of human relations, could in the same way be reduced to relatively simple mechanical laws akin to those of the physical sciences. It seemed to many in the eighteenth century that Newton had provided the key that would unlock all the mysteries of the universe. Man's task was simply to determine what the underlying laws of nature were and, by use of his reason, adjust to them so that he could live in harmony with his world. The first half of the eighteenth century thus became a confident Age of Reason, in which it was assumed that man was an "enlightened" creature (hence the term "Enlightenment" used to describe the period) whose power to perfect himself was unlimited. No longer were men to be thought of as inherently wicked beings, imperfect and infected with original sin—men, whether they were good or evil, were products of the environment in which they lived. Evil men resulted from evils in their surroundings and bad institutions or wicked superstitions inherited from their unenlightened forebears. What man needed above all to progress (and the word "progress" was one of the great watchwords of the Enlightenment) was freedom to develop his powers of reason and to reform the evils in the world about him so that, as he improved materially, he would also improve morally. He had to have liberty to express himself freely, to worship as he wished, and to choose those things his reason told him were good. As a consequence, the great writers of the Enlightenment, particularly in France, were not only strong social critics but also defenders of a philosophy of "enlightened individualism."

The influence of these basic ideas reached out to touch every kind of thought. Let us now look at some of the most important of their effects.

1. RELIGION

In the area of religious belief the most important single effect stemming from the scientific revolution and the Enlightenment was a weakening of faith among the intellectual classes of Europe. It had not been the intention of many of the great scientific thinkers of the seventeenth century to destroy Christian theology or to weaken the basis of belief. Many of them—Newton for example—were profoundly religious men. Inevitably, however, some of the things they said, simply because their statements seemed to be at variance with teachings long accepted as orthodox, created serious tensions between themselves and

in Christ alone; Moravian Brethren in Germany who reorganized themselves in 1732; Israel B. Eliezer (Baal-Schem-Tov), 1700–1760, founder of the devout pietistic Jewish group known as the Hasidim.

2. POLITICAL THEORY

Just as John Locke was the leading proponent of the philosophy of the Enlightenment, so he was also in large measure the founder of its political theory. That is not to say that everyone in the eighteenth century accepted what Locke had to say without question. Nevertheless, Locke's *Two Treatises of Government*, published in 1690, but probably written between 1679 and 1681, came to be widely accepted during the eighteenth century as an apologetic for the English Revolution of 1688. In brief, Locke argued that government (including even kings) was responsible to the governed as a consequence of a mythical contract entered into when society was first formed. If the contract was broken by the ruler, the community had the right to rebel. The idea was based upon a questionable historical hypothesis but, nonetheless, had a wide influence on the thought of eighteenth-century Europe. The notion of limited power was carried over into French thought by Montesquieu (1689–1755) in his *Spirit of Laws*, 1748. C. A. Helvetius (1715–1771) sought to give political theory a "scientific" basis by arguing that the only rational standard of conduct was one based upon the "greatest good for the greatest number;" he published *De l'esprit (Of the Spirit)* in 1758. J. J. Rousseau (1712–1778) in his *Social Contract*, 1762, put forward the idea that society as a whole is possessed of a "general will," which directs the affairs of government. Publication of the *Encyclopedia* under the editorship of Denis Diderot (1713–1784), a work that summarized the ideals of the Enlightenment, 1751–1765. Marquis de Condorcet (1743–1794) best expressed the Enlightenment's faith in human progress in his *Progress of the Human Spirit*, 1794.

An important result of the political theorizing of the Enlightenment was its spread into the transatlantic world of North America. There in the last third of the eighteenth century it helped to shape revolutionary attitudes that made possible the revolt of the thirteen British colonies against the authority of the British crown.

3. ECONOMIC THEORY

Western man has long attempted to understand the complex economic interrelationships of the material world in which people live. Just who first began to speculate about the economic circumstances of European man is impossible to say, though there is evidence of such thinking as far back as the Middle Ages. The sixteenth and seventeenth centuries, however, saw the first major attempts to explain economic relationships in a compre-

churchmen of all denominations. A great part of the difficulty arose from the fact that by stressing the importance, the permanence, and the unchanging nature of the physical laws that controlled the universe, the scientific thinkers of the period appeared to imply that God was only a sort of watchmaker who made the universe and set it in motion, and then left it to its own devices. Such an implication challenged the stories of divine intervention in human affairs as related by scripture and the Christian tradition—miracles became impossible because they were in violation of an inviolable natural law. Even more disturbing, such a mechanistic implication made men wonder about the accuracy of scripture itself. Impelled by doubts, many scholars turned to reexamine the Bible in a new critical light, and their findings inevitably raised new questions. From this dilemma of reason and faith men found various escapes. Some denied its existence and reaffirmed their traditional beliefs. Others, most notably the school of philosopher-theologians known as the Deists, sought a form of compromise in which God was deemed not a personal deity in the Christian sense but a remote, impersonal "Supreme Being." A few went the whole way to atheism and argued that the universe, which seemed on the basis of physical law to have existed through all eternity, had no creator but was a kind of timeless machine existing without a beginning or an end.

2. POLITICAL THEORY

The political theory of the Enlightenment derived from the fundamental belief that man is a creature of his environment who needs only to improve his surroundings in order to progress toward earthly perfection. In those parts of Europe—England for example—where the state and society seemed conducive to a certain amount of individual freedom and where the power of rational choice appeared not to be markedly restricted by social traditions and political institutions, the ideals and aspirations of the Enlightenment strengthened the social order. In France, on the other hand, because of growing discontent with inequities in taxation, bureaucratic inefficiency, and the entrenched position of the nobility, the ideas of the Enlightenment took on a revolutionary cast. Furthermore, the arguments of the French *philosophes* (philosophers) were reinforced in popular thinking by the successive military defeats sustained by France at the hands of England during the first half of the eighteenth century. As a consequence of these, Frenchmen inevitably asked what it was that gave England her advantage and concluded that it lay in the superiority of England's enlightened institutions and traditions. Leading thinkers like Voltaire and Montesquieu became ardent admirers of all things English, which

hensive way as men began to be curious about the reasons for certain kinds of economic occurrences like inflated prices, the slow rise of wages, the flow of metallic money from one region to another, and recurring periods of prosperity or depression. At first much of the writing was empirical, in that men sought only to describe what they observed without drawing any fundamental conclusions or trying to discover any general laws about the economic process. Perhaps the first great economic thinker of early modern Europe was Jean Bodin (1530–1596), French lawyer and political philosopher, who in 1588 undertook to explain sixteenth-century inflation in a work entitled *Responses to the Paradoxes of the Sieur de Malestroit*. During the century following, however, a group of British thinkers broadened the bases of economic inquiry by making the first moves toward creating a system capable of explanation and prediction, which are the characteristics of a true "science." The man who strove most explicitly to put economics on a "scientific" basis was Sir William Petty (1623–1687), who in his *Political Arithmetick* (1671) and subsequent essays tried to apply the methods of mathematics to economic matters. The major attempt to formulate a scientific economics came in the eighteenth century with the spread of the assumption that economics was based on discernible general laws and could therefore be studied like any other science.

The belief that there were laws governing economic activity was first given coherent form in the writings of the French physiocrats, whose most important writer, Dr. Francis Quesnay (1694–1774), published influential articles in the *Encyclopedia*, 1756–1757, and his major work, *Tableau économique*, in 1756. The essence of physiocratic doctrine was a belief in the "natural order" of economic activity. Quesnay and his followers argued that wealth was not gold and silver but sprang from production and flowed through the nation to replenish the whole of society. The difficulty with physiocracy, however, was that its adherents insisted that agriculture alone produced wealth and that merchants and manufacturers only manipulated it for their own ends. Under physiocratic influences A. R. J. Turgot (1727–1781), the great French finance minister, published his *Reflections on the Formation and Distribution of Wealth*, 1766. Adam Smith, 1723–1790, after a visit to France in 1764–1766 incorporated a number of physiocratic ideas into his *Wealth of Nations*, 1776. Smith's great work was not simply a statement of laissez-faire principles. He was concerned to show what the mechanism was by which society functions. In explanation he formulated the laws of the market. What he strove to demonstrate was the way in which all men by pursuing their own interests would seek, as if led by an "invisible hand," the end "which is most agreeable to the interest of the

they held up to Frenchmen as enlightened models. From England, too, were imported certain social and political theories originally developed by Thomas Hobbes (1588–1679) and John Locke (1632–1704) which, in French hands, were to become dangerous intellectual weapons.

Basically, however, the political theory of the Enlightenment, while it varied from individual to individual, held that as a rational being man had the right to create his own political institutions if those already in existence did not conform to the standards of his reason. This view did not necessarily lead to democracy, since, in the opinion of many *philosophes*, not all men had reached the level of rationality needed to make democracy work. It did imply, however—though many thinkers preferred to trust an enlightened monarch—that all those possessed of reasoning power, knowledge, and education could or should have some part in governing themselves. This belief was capable of ultimate enormous expansion and could lead to revolutionary conclusions.

3. ECONOMIC THEORY

Just as the physical universe had its laws, so too it was assumed during the Enlightenment that human social and economic relationships were also governed by laws that it was the duty of the rational man to seek out and understand. Under the influence of this kind of thinking a great deal of new attention was devoted to understanding man's relations with his material environment and with other people. To this end, society was studied as never before, and for the first time a serious attempt was made to create what we now call the "social sciences."

The most popular and famous of these many attempts was the work of Adam Smith, whose *Wealth of Nations* (1776) was to become the bible of the new social science of "political economy" (later to be known as "economics"). Smith was not merely a theorist of the Enlightenment, however. He was also an antagonist of certain economic theories and practices, like the restrictive system of mercantilism, which he felt were dangerously limiting the economic growth of European society. The theory of mercantilism, whose greatest exponent had been the French finance minister Colbert (1619–1683), was derived from the belief that all trade and manufacturing had to be strictly controlled in the interests of the state. Commercial activity under mercantilism was the analog of warfare, in which a nation strove to amass wealth by accumulating bullion (gold and silver), or by exporting goods of greater money value than it imported from its neighbors. Against this view (though he did feel that the state had the right to

whole society." Thomas Malthus (1766–1834) in his *Essay on the Principle of Population*, 1798, challenged the optimism of the eighteenth century by arguing that population always tends to far outstrip the means of subsistence.

4. ENLIGHTENED DESPOTISM

Frederick the Great of Prussia (1740–1786) described himself as "the first servant of the state"; worked to improve the economic conditions of Prussia; was friendly with Voltaire and other philosophers of the Enlightenment; spoke French in preference to German; and interested himself in philosophy and the arts.

Catherine the Great of Russia (1762–1796) patronized the French *philosophes*; codified Russian laws; and interested herself in the philosophy of the Enlightenment.

Joseph II of Austria (1765–1790), one of the few rulers who really believed in enlightened despotism, tried to institute popular education; reformed the legal code; and promoted religious toleration even in the face of strong opposition from his own subjects.

impose some restrictions when national interests were at stake), Smith argued that the economic world was governed by a body of laws all its own that had nothing to do with politics or the policies of states. Economic systems were controlled by natural laws, which could not be flouted at the whim of human beings. Men should be left free to follow their own enlightened self-interest in economic matters and, in so doing, would be acting in harmony with those laws. To facilitate this freedom, every form of restriction, tariff, or other barrier to unfettered trade should be abolished, and men should be let alone (laissez-faire) to engage in economic activity. The purpose of government was to provide social stability, security of life and property, and enforcement of contracts. If it did these things and nothing more, men, left to themselves to seek their own rational economic ends, would also ultimately serve the welfare of society as a whole.

4. ENLIGHTENED DESPOTISM: THE POLITICAL EFFECT OF THE ENLIGHTENMENT

With the wide dissemination of the teachings of the Enlightenment, eighteenth-century Europe witnessed the rise of a new phenomenon known as "enlightened despotism." To a large extent, the system of enlightened despotism was only an extension of the older forms of absolute monarchy; but it was absolute monarchy with a difference. By the middle of the eighteenth century it was no longer fashionable, even among kings, to insist that their rule was justified solely by inheritance or divine right. The sovereign, following the example of the kings of Prussia, was the "first servant of the state" and was obligated to provide for the general welfare of his people by giving them efficient government, reforms when needed, and equal justice. In short, the enlightened despot, by endeavoring to rule according to the dictates of reason, justified his authority on the purely secular grounds of usefulness. Furthermore, under the influence of the prevailing ideas, he often promoted reforms that were opposed by large numbers of his subjects. For this reason, the rule of the enlightened despot might be called paternal in the sense that change was accomplished for the good of the people whether they liked it or not. But the enlightened despots were not necessarily motivated by the prevailing ideas. Many of their reforms were carried out as a means of organizing the resources of their kingdoms for greater efficiency in waging war against their neighbors and not with the welfare of their subjects in mind.

5. THE TRANSATLANTIC REVOLUTION, 1760–1815

Causes: (1) spread of literacy fostered consciousness of the possibility of social transformation; (2) a literate class of property owners—middle class or bourgeoisie—emerged, with enlarged aspirations for political power; (3) enormous increase of European population during the eighteenth century created problems of subsistence and employment with which the state was increasingly unable to cope; (4) slow but continual rise in costs affected both individuals and governments, thus giving rise to numerous fiscal crises.

5.   THE TRANSATLANTIC REVOLUTION, 1760–1815

In the second half of the eighteenth century there began a movement —whose best example is the French Revolution—to broaden the bases of mass influence in European society and to eliminate at least some of the distinctions of rank and status that for centuries had characterized the hierarchically organized social systems of most European states. Why such a movement with such widespread effects began at that moment in time is difficult to say. Surely one of the major reasons was that people increasingly expected that life could be bettered in a great variety of ways by social and political action. Certainly the spread of discontent that engendered such feelings was caused to a very large extent by the flow of ideas from one region to another as a consequence of the significant increase in literacy during the course of the eighteenth century.

Whatever the cause of the transformation, many historians now argue that this "Great Revolution of the West" ushered in a new era during which the problems and aspirations of the masses became increasingly a major concern of western societies.

chapter ten

The Western World in 1700: A Summary and Conclusion

THE ESSENTIAL MOVEMENT

By the year 1700, Western civilization had reached a point in its historic development where it was possible to forecast the pattern of later events. Political, scientific, and philosophical events were in train that did not culminate until the end of the century. Indeed, almost all the distinctive qualities that were to give wealth and power to the West during the next 250 years had already begun to evolve out of the complex of European life. Europeans had conquered and settled vast areas beyond the seas. Scientific ideas, technological skills, and productive techniques, though they were to bring about an industrial revolution in the century after 1700, had advanced to a stage where the West for the first time in its history produced more goods and wealth than any other area on earth. The European mind, strongly influenced by the ideas of the scientific revolution of the seventeenth century, was already confidently conscious of the possibility that all the "big ques tions" about man and the universe might at last be answered. In the sphere of politics the state had reached a point in its evolution where more was expected of it than ever before: in response to this expectation it had expanded both its authority and bureaucracy but had been less successful in expanding its revenues. For a long time, too, the state

169

had confronted a growing complexity in its relations with those whom it ruled, and some European countries had already passed through the turmoil of civil war and revolution that was symptomatic of this difficulty.

In the light of these developments let us now turn our attention once again to the five major themes discussed in the introduction to this volume and see just how each of them had evolved up to the opening of the eighteenth century.

A. HUMAN MANIPULATION OF THE WORLD OF NATURE (THE MATERIAL ENVIRONMENT)

At the beginning of the eighteenth century western man had come a long way in his struggle to mitigate the adverse influences of his environment. He had not yet discovered new sources of energy to supplant those usually found in nature—i.e., wind, water, and human or animal power; and it is doubtful whether any of his inventions or discoveries for some thousands of years were as fundamentally significant as those made during the Neolithic Revolution. Yet, despite reverses and periods when his cultural achievements fell below those of preceding generations, he had refined the techniques by which he won his subsistence and added to the details of his varied knowledge in many ways.

In one important respect, however, man's achievements had not followed a path of continuous progress. With the collapse of Rome and the disintegration of a unified Mediterranean civilization the historic continuity of human knowledge, though not entirely broken, was very much attenuated in many regions that had been part of the Roman Empire (and particularly in those inhabited by the Germanic peoples). For some centuries there was no longer an extensive or consistent interchange or expansion of ideas and techniques throughout the region we now know as Europe; and for that reason the years between about A.D. 500 and 1000 to some extent must be thought of as the Dark Ages. Yet we should bear in mind that learning, even in the classical sense, was never entirely lost and that there were forces at work during those centuries that deny the stereotyped view of the period as one of unrelieved ignorance.

Here and there in isolated places significant technological advances were made; but knowledge of them spread slowly, and frequently skills were lost from one generation to another because people who knew of them were limited in number or lived in places remote from the areas of greatest population. What this era lacked perhaps more than anything else was institutional continuity of the kind that preserves and conveys knowledge from one generation to the next. The great universities of later medieval Europe did not yet exist, and the church had not yet become the highly rationalized and cohesive international organization that it would be in the High Middle Ages. While it is true that the Latin church through its monastic centers helped to keep "the lamp of learning alight," it had not regained the traditions and efficiency of the Roman administrative system or the centralized authority that had disappeared with the disintegration of the Western Empire.

Although the causes are not yet entirely clear to us, it is known that some time toward the end of the tenth or beginning of the eleventh century there began a series of movements that reinvigorated the life of the West and ushered in another period of expansion. Population growth may have played a part in it, but this we cannot know with certainty because we lack statistics. Furthermore, mere population growth has never been a guarantee of resultant intellectual or technical expansion; in fact in many societies it has forced down living standards and caused intellectual stagnation. Undoubtedly, the Cluniac and later Gregorian reforms (so called after Pope Gregory VII) played a part in this change by revitalizing that greatest of medieval institutions, the church, which in turn spread the new leaven through medieval society. This effect may best be seen in the founding of new monastic orders and the growth of universities. As important as any of these was an economic and technological expansion marked, on the one hand, by the founding of new cities and the growth of old ones and, on the other, by an apparent increase in agricultural and other productivity. In this area, too, we are at loss to explain all the reasons for sudden vitality. It may be that the eleventh century was simply a time when a great many developments reaching far back into the western past and not easily identified by historians began to have a cumulative effect. Some historians now believe that the most important cause of this great economic change was the growth of the early feudal state, whch, though relatively weak and ineffective in many ways, provided the degree of security and political stability needed to stimulate economic activity.

Still we must not exaggerate the effects of this expansion by assuming that it led at once to a broad extension of human control over the material environment. Western technology, until about the fifteenth century, lagged behind that of some Middle Eastern and oriental societies; and western man, like everyone else, could and did suffer horribly from natural catastrophes over which he had little or no control and whose consequences often altered his way of life in curiously unpredictable ways. Year in and year out, with fearsome regularity, he was visited by plagues. Men sometimes died in such numbers—as in the Black Death of 1348–1349—that the very structure of society was altered and the course of history undoubtedly changed. Famines were a common part of the human lot, and even the richest societies were seldom far removed from the danger of harvest failure and the horrors of mass starvation. In most European cities such elemental methods of disease prevention as drainage, sewerage, and pure water supply, which had been known to the ancients, were not used extensively until well along in the eighteenth and nineteenth centuries.

Nevertheless, the upward curve of scientific and technological achievement during the years between 1000 and 1700 was impressive. New methods of navigation and ship construction made possible longer and safer voyages. Although the development of military technology enabled Europeans to kill one another in larger numbers, it also put an end to the danger, ever present until the end of the Middle Ages, of outside conquest by Turks or Mongols who might have destroyed Western civilization. Extensive engineering projects like the canals and dikes of Holland and the great swamp-drainage undertakings of England and France brought large areas of previously unused land under cultivation. In medicine, advances in the study of anatomy and bodily functions prepared the way for even greater successes in the future. But it was in the growth of scientific thought that the greatest potential for the future was achieved, for the seventeenth century was a time of genius that saw the formulation of the basic scientific hypotheses that were to transform the Western World during the next 250 years and make its achievements unique and greater than any in previous history. By 1700 men already believed that science might well be the means of extending the "empire of man over nature" as never before.

B. BELIEF IN AN ORDERED, PURPOSEFUL UNIVERSE AND HISTORICAL PROGRESS

With scientific and technological advance, western man by 1700 had become more and more convinced that nature was governed by laws that gave order to the universe and could be made to work for man's benefit. Moreover, he was also convinced that these laws, as the discoveries of Galileo and Newton seemed to prove, could be comprehended by the human mind.

This faith in an ordered universe and the power of the mind, though very much intensified as a result of the scientific achievements of the seventeenth century, was no new thing in the history of Western civilization. Its beginnings went back to the earliest Greek thinkers who assumed the existence of order beneath all the shifting, diverse phenomena of the everyday world. In large measure this belief was responsible for the development of Greek mathematics and the Greek attempt, best exemplified in the thought of Plato, to explain the cosmos and the relationships of the world of matter to the world of ideas. Indeed, it is the persistence of this Greek view of things, later carried over into Christian thought, that has come to be looked upon as one of the unique and significant elements in Western civilization. Without such a faith western man might not have attempted to formulate the laws of modern science. Here, as in a number of other areas, the West owes much to the High Middle Ages, the period that was for long assumed by historians to have been one of darkness and ignorance. For the medieval philosophers, though they worked within the restrictive framework of Christian belief, helped to preserve the tradition that the universe was ordered and rational by incorporating much of Greek philosophy, and particularly the writings of Aristotle, into Christian thought. In so doing they performed an important service for the West, even while they tended to hold too slavishly to the letter of Aristotle's teachings and thus, in some respects, held up the development of scientific thought during the fifteenth and sixteenth centuries: they kept alive the basic Greek way of looking at the world.

For long the significance of this service was overlooked by historians and scientists who thought of the Scientific Revolution as a complete reaction against the medieval way of looking at things. They held that the Middle Ages accepted truth on the basis of revealed authority, while science is based solely upon observation and experiment; therefore, the modern scientific method as it has evolved since the seventeenth century is the very antithesis of medieval thought. But it is not antithesis, for the scientific method is made up of *two* important elements: one is empiricism (i.e., observation and experiment), which scientists have regarded as absolutely essential to scientific advance since the days of Galileo; the other is rationalism (i.e., the assumption that nature is governed by laws). Without this rational element, which was preserved from the western past by the medieval philosophers, the scientific method and the scientific way of looking at the world could not have come into being.

With the emergence of this new scientific way of thought, western man's notion of purpose in history also changed. Just as the achievements of the Scientific Revolution increased his intellectual self-confidence, so in many ways it also increased his confidence that history was a steady progression toward moral and material perfection. Like the western belief in an ordered universe, this idea was not entirely new. Both Judaism and Christianity had taught that humanity was moving toward a far-off rendezvous—a last judgment—at the end of time. But while Christians had believed in man's perfectibility, they had also been taught that such perfection was to be found only in the life hereafter.

About 1700 the essentially Christian view that humanity was moving toward the last judgment was transformed into the view that men were moving toward perfectibility in this world. The new view did not claim that each man would attain perfection in his own lifetime. Perfection was something attainable by the human race as a whole only after a long period of time had elapsed. Each generation, by adding to the sum of human knowledge, would raise mankind stage by stage toward perfection; for this was the law of progress. This new doctrine taught that progress was inevitable; never again would mankind relapse into barbarism, because human knowledge and reason were now sufficiently advanced to keep history moving in one direction—forward. In this view, change was neither bad nor meaningless. On the contrary, it was always good and purposeful. It was progress and therefore good, and anything that deterred progress was bad. Thus armed with a belief that history was on his side, western man now confidently assumed that there was nothing beyond his ultimate comprehension or accomplishment.

C. THE EXPANSION OF EUROPE

At the end of the seventeenth century the process of European expansion had already reached a stage where it was no longer a development of merely European but of worldwide significance. By the year 1700, thousands of Europeans had already ceased to be inhabitants of Europe and had taken up permanent residence overseas. In some cases this residence had extended over so many generations that Europe was a remote ancestral homeland far removed from the immediate concerns and interests of many overseas colonists. As yet no area of European settlement was politically or culturally independent of Europe, but the time of political separation for some of them was not far off. Furthermore, the European economy was already tied into a large global system of economic relations upon which Europe depended for a significant part of its commerce and for some of its material resources.

This state of affairs was the result of five different but closely related developments, each of which we must now examine briefly.

1. GROWTH OF POPULATION

Since most European states had no regular census-taking procedures until the nineteenth century, historians and demographers (population experts) have had to rely on somewhat indirect evidence for their estimates of population change or growth before the year 1800. The informed consensus, however, is that the population of Europe down to about 1650 was increasing but that its growth was slow in contrast to its enormous increase after that date.

Nevertheless, all evidence indicates that most countries had much larger populations in the year 1700 than they had in the year 1000. England, for example, is estimated to have had a population of slightly more than one million persons near the end of the eleventh century (1086); by 1700 the estimated figure had grown to about 6 million. While these absolute figures are small in modern terms, the rate of growth is fairly substantial. Even more important, however, was the enormous growth that most demographers believe began about the year 1650. Since that time—and the forces of increase were obviously at work in 1700—there has taken place not an expansion but an explosion of Europeans. While it is true that today the populations of Asia and parts of Africa are numerically larger than those of Europe or of areas settled by Europeans overseas, their historic rate of increase does not appear to have been nearly so high. If we look again at England, the most striking example of this increase, we can see how almost unbelievably high the rate of growth has been. In 1700 there were probably fewer than 10 million English-speaking persons in all the world. By 1950 that number had grown to more than 250 million.

For both the earlier and later rates of growth there have been a number of explanations. One very probable reason that European population grew even before 1650 was an increase in food supply. Another was the greater security provided by the expanded police power of the centralized state. Preventive medicine and extensive improvments in technology, though by no means negligible factors, were not yet developed enough to have the effects that they were to have at a later date. In both periods—before and after 1650—the factor of living space may also have to be taken into account. The European continent, with some few excepted areas, had an abundance of land that could be made to produce sufficient food for its people with the agricultural techniques available. Moreover, Europeans were also moving into sparsely settled overseas regions where their skills could be utilized for the production of wealth and the necessities of life even more successfully.

As we noted earlier, however, mere population growth alone is not proof of the success of a civilization in terms of what it can offer to its peoples. The great advantage that western man was to have as his numbers grew after 1650 lay in his ability, first to create new scientific ideas and technological skills, which in turn enabled him to exploit previously unused natural resources; and, second, in his ability to use his superior military and technological power to conquer and settle vast overseas areas. As a result, population growth had a stimulating effect because it did not overtax the natural resources or outstrip man's ability to exploit them. Had he lacked these abilities, the lot of western man might have been that of his fellow humans in countries like China or India, where population increase, at least prior to our own time, was not accompanied by a general rise in the standard of living. As it was, however, the Western world in 1700 stood on the verge of a period of growth during which both population and the level of general subsistence rose simultaneously.

2. RISE OF CITIES AND TOWNS (INCREASING URBANIZATION)

The rise of cities and towns was another important characteristic of the general expansion of Europe that began about the year 1000. City origins, like the origins of the expansionist movement as a whole, are somewhat obscure, but it is generally conceded that a revival of trade was the most important cause of the revival of urban life in the West. Not all cities, however, came into existence for commercial reasons. Some, as in Italy, were Roman survivals. Others, particularly in the north of Europe, grew up around fortresses, cathedrals, or abbeys, which were important centers of regional administration. In the long run, however, even these were sustained and augmented by trade.

The effects of urban growth on Western civilization have been so many and so diverse that it is difficult to summarize them. Some historians have gone so far as to suggest that the influence of urbanization has been more important than any other. Though the point may be argued, there is no doubt that the spread of vast centers of urban population has changed the living habits and even the ideas of modern man in many significant ways.

In the year 1700, however, European towns and cities had not yet achieved the preponderance of numbers and wealth that they possess in our own time. At the opening of the eighteenth century, it is believed, only two cities in all Europe—London and Paris—had populations of 500,000 or more and thus approached in size and in the complexity of their problems the cities of the twentieth century. In almost every state of Europe agriculture was the most important economic activity and commanded the efforts and attention of by far the largest part of the population.

One of the major reasons why city life had not yet become as important or as concentrated as it was to become later was that industrial production was still widely scattered in small handicraft units under what is known variously as the cottage, domestic, or "putting out" system. Individuals and families working in their own homes had no need to live in cities, as they later would after the centralized factory came into existence. Most towns and cities, though not all, were commercial rather than manufacturing centers. Furthermore, many inhabitants of cities, right down through the seventeenth century, tilled their fields during the day and lived inside city walls only at night.

As a consequence, the European way of life in 1700 was still overwhelmingly rural. This does not mean, however, that society had not changed very radically in the centuries since 1000. The rise of towns had transformed the economic and social relations of European society in many ways. Since the very existence of populated centers requires that the agricultural system produce a surplus that can be used to feed those urban people who do not produce food for themselves, there were created throughout western Europe market areas where the rural inhabitants had changed their agricultural techniques to conform to the needs of the towns. In so doing, the rural producer also changed the system of feudal-manorial relations. Serfs, as they accumulated a surplus of money, were able to transform (commute) their manorial obligations into money payments and often to purchase their freedom from serfdom. Though the processes by which this change took place differed in rate from country to country (in some parts of Europe it was not completed until the nineteenth century), by the year 1700 the restrictive system of manorial relations had markedly declined.

The growth of cities also had other important general effects. The commercial activities of the townsmen forced them to live outside the customary arrangements of feudal society. Trade required freedom of movement, a different conception of property rights, and a system of law opposed to that of the manor. By striving to win these, the town dweller broadened the area of individual action and thus indirectly helped to expand intellectual and political freedom. And, finally, the new wealth of the towns eased the rigidity of the feudal class structure and created a new social mobility by making it possible for men to rise more easily on the social scale.

This last development brought into existence a new group within the European social order, sometimes called the burgesses, the bourgeoisie, or, more loosely, the middle classes. The immediate political importance of this new social element has often been exaggeratd by historians, but there is no doubt that these men and the commercial form of wealth they represented did have significant long-range effects on European historical development. By 1700 they were a well-established part of the European scene, and their ideas and influence were to be felt increasingly during the 250 years that followed.

3.   COLONIZATION IN EUROPE AND OVERSEAS

Though we usually associate migration and colonization with European overseas expansion, Europeans had actually been migrating and colonizing within Europe itself long before Columbus's discovery. From the tenth through the sixteenth centuries there was a steady movement outward from the more heavily populated regions of Europe into sparsely settled underdeveloped border regions or into areas occupied by non-Christians. Two of these expansionist efforts—i.e., the Christian crusades against the Saracens in the Middle East and the conquest of the Greek empire of Byzantium in the thirteenth century—ended ultimately in failure, but elsewhere Europeans were more successful. Beginning in the twelfth century Englishmen undertook the conquest of Ireland, Scotland, and Wales—the "Celtic fringes" of the British Isles. By the end of the Middle Ages they had overcome the Welsh, partially conquered the Irish, and failed in their efforts to subdue the Scots. In Spain the Christian kingdoms gradually pushed back the earlier Moslem conquerors until in 1491 the last independent Islamic state (Cordova) fell to Ferdinand and Isabella. Farther east, German settlers from the tenth century onward passed over the Elbe and Oder rivers to conquer and Christianize the pagan Slavs of the Baltic region. As the centralized power of the various European states increased, all the peripheral regions were forced to acknowledge the sovereignty of the new nation-states.

Far more dramatic and of more obvious significance in terms of world history was the expansion of Europe overseas. Never again until —and if—space travel becomes possible will men have the same experience that Europeans had in the 200 years after the discovery of the western hemisphere. Even more remarkable than the fact of discovery, however, were the mass migrations that led to permanent settlement and the transference of European ways and traditions to regions far removed from Europe itself. No other movement on such a scale had ever been undertaken in all the world's history. Some notion of the magnitude of this migration may be had if we remember that in the period between 1607, when the first permanent English settlement in North America was made at Jamestown, and 1776, when the American Revolution began, the population of British North America increased, largely by immigration, from about 100 persons to an estimated 2.5 million. What was true of England's colonies was also true, though to a lesser extent, of the colonies of other European powers.

4. THE REVOLUTION IN THE TECHNIQUES OF PRODUCTION AND TRANSPORTATION

While it is true that the most spectacular industrial advances of modern times were made from the latter part of the eighteenth century onward, we now know that for some centuries before that time numerous changes had been taking place in European economic life, which made the development during the eighteenth century far less revolutionary than has sometimes been thought. Even so early as the thirteenth and fourteenth centuries Europe had developed specialized productive skills, most notably in textiles, which had begun to shift the balance of trade with the Orient in Europe's favor. In short, European products of all kinds came to be in greater demand; as a result, Europe began to sell more abroad than was imported, a transformation that helped to increase the accumulation of capital (see below). By the sixteenth and seventeenth centuries a slow but steady improvement in the technology of production brought on an early "industrial revolution," particularly in the north of Europe. Between 1540 and 1640 the English—followed by the Dutch and the Swedes—enormously increased their production of textiles by expanding the "putting out" or domestic system of household manufacture; at the same time they accomplished a revolution in the use of coal and iron. Evidence also indicates that by the middle of the seventeenth century England and Sweden between them produced nearly as much iron as all the rest of Europe together, despite the fact that the combined population of the two countries was only about 8 million.

More immediately significant for overseas expansion and commerce, however, were the improvements in navigational skill and shipbuilding technology to which every maritime nation of Europe contributed from the fifteenth century onward. The compass, the rudder, the astrolabe, and the true chart made it possible for European ships to sail more quickly and precisely from one point on the globe to another. Improvement in shipbuilding made it possible to transport larger numbers of men and goods in relative safety. What was most important, however, was that in the process navigators and mariners made use of a generalized intellectual skill inherent in the whole long tradition of European thought. The first to do so successfully were the Portuguese and the Spaniards. When Prince Henry the Navigator

(1394–1460) ordered his ship captains to keep exact logbooks of information gained from their voyages and to contribute that information to a common pool of knowledge, he was demonstrating a European quality that no other society possessed to quite the same degree. Prince Henry was making use of accumulated practical knowledge in a rationalized way for the benefit of the inexperienced and in behalf of later generations. The increase and continuity of such knowledge helped to give Europeans a means of discovery and, later, of colonization far beyond anything known in previous societies. With this development, large-scale transplantation of people from Europe to the most distant parts of the earth became possible. One other element was needed to make it feasible: capital wealth.

5. THE GROWTH OF CAPITAL WEALTH

In any society, economic expansion (i.e., the growth of total economic production, which alone can raise living standards) while it depends upon a number of factors, cannot occur unless that society possesses two fundamental things. First, it must have a large body of skilled manpower; and, second, it must have an accumulation of capital. The word "capital" has been given many meanings, but in precise economic terms it is commonly defined as "produced wealth used productively for gain." In this sense, capital is always distinguished from commodities like food, clothes, automobiles, or houses, which, though they have an economic value and may be necessary for an individual's well-being, are not always used directly to produce more wealth. Capital in its simplest form is thus an accumulation of what we call "savings," which are left over from income after all other needs have been satisfied and which may be employed for gainful purposes. For most people the easiest and most obvious way of employing such capital savings is to put them in a bank where they will draw interest. Before savings can earn interest, however, the bank's directors must make use of them in productive ways by investing them in business enterprises or in loans. In this respect, the banker acts as a manager of his depositors' money, and the individual saver is freed of the responsibility for looking after his capital himself. Since banks, in most cases, are fairly safe places to put capital, the interest rate on that capital in return for safety is always relatively low. For those who hope for a larger return, which often calls for a certain amount of speculative risk, the stock market offers another area of capital investment. There individuals keep a somewhat more direct control over their savings by purchasing stocks (capital shares that entitle those who buy them to shares of a company's earnings if profits permit) or bonds (certificates of indebtedness on which interest is paid and that are secured by a company's tangible assets). And, finally, there is a third and much more direct way of employing capital savings. That is by using them to start a business venture of one's own.

All of these methods—and many more—are so much a part of western man's economic experience that he seldom thinks about their historic significance. Often he simply assumes that they are a result of the natural order of things and that they must inevitably appear in any society where wealth has increased to a certain point. Unfortunately, as the experience of many twentieth-century underdeveloped societies indicates, such an evolution is by no means automatic. In many instances it is the result of a complex of social factors that almost no societies outside the area of Western civilization have possessed to a significant degree.

The first of these factors is surplus product; the accumulation of capital savings, whether undertaken by individuals as it is in western democratic countries or by the state as it is in countries like the Soviet Union, requires that a society not use all of its income for immediate consumption. In other words, its people cannot be living at a level of bare subsistence but must produce a surplus over and above their ordinary needs. Where the level of productive techniques is too low or where natural resources are insufficient, the lack of surplus becomes a difficult problem, which can be solved only by borrowing capital from some outside source or by further depressing the living standards of society until a surplus is created.

The accumulation of surplus, however, is only the first step in the process of economic expansion. Opportunity to use the surplus productively is a second social factor. A method or methods for deciding what use the surplus should be applied to is a third. In collectivist societies where the state in effect controls all economic surplus, it also determines how that surplus will be used. Throughout most of the Western world, however, the decision as to how savings will be employed has been left up to the individual. Wherever this latter course has been followed, certain other things then have to happen if the productive capacity of society is to be expanded by capital investment. Of primary importance to the individual investor is the security of his savings—a fourth social factor. Even when he speculates by putting his money into a new venture, he likes to feel that his chances of getting a return on it are at least reasonably good, apart from ordinary economic mischance. He must accordingly have faith in the political and social stability of the society in which he lives—or invests. If the state is in danger of overthrow or if external invasion threatens or if the head of state can seize his money for capricious reasons, then the potential investor is likely to keep his money at home in a strong box under the bed. Furthermore, there must also exist a means whereby investor and entrepreneur can be brought together. In the Western world this means has been supplied by banks, brokerage houses and stock exchanges, all of which are devices evolved over a long period of time for the easier circulation of capital. Finally, not only must speculative investors have a sense of confidence in their society but also they must be willing to forgo immediate economic gains in the expectation of greater ones at some future time.

By the year 1700 most of these conditions existed in a number of western European states, but particularly in England and Holland. To a large extent these conditions were the culmination of a process commonly described as the "commercial revolution," by which the capital wealth of Europeans had greatly increased from the twelfth century onward. This revolution was the result of several causes. One was improvement in agricultural techniques coupled with the rise of towns (whose needs had prompted the rural areas to increase food production above the level of subsistence), which had helped to create productive surpluses in agriculture. Second, the growing power of the state, especially in the national monarchies, provided a stable social and political setting in which men could have confidence that their economic plans had a reasonable chance of coming to fruition. And, third, the development of improved business practices and organization as well as the growth of banks and stock exchanges had twofold effect. On the one hand, an organizational innovation like the limited-liability joint-stock company, by sharing out the risk of loss among many stockholders, greatly reduced the danger of sudden bankruptcy and thus made a greater number of people more willing to participate in large-scale ventures. At the same time, the rise of banks and exchanges made it easier to mobilize large amounts of capital at lower rates of interest, which, in turn, made possible the expansion of mercantile and industrial operations. So significant was this last development that some economic historians now believe it to have been almost as important a factor in causing the later industrial revolution as the invention of the steam engine.

In summing up, there are three important effects of the growth of capital wealth that we need to keep in mind. (1) With the creation and circulation of capital the Western world hit upon a method of continuously expanding production and, in so doing, made it possible for a larger number of people than ever before to enjoy economic benefits formerly reserved for the very few. (2) Because this wealth existed side by side with an improved technology, Europeans were able to undertake overseas colonization and settlement on an unprecedented scale. And (3) the investment of wealth in all parts of the world during the eighteenth and nineteenth centuries gave to western Europe an economic as well as a political power that reached around the world.

D. THE PROBLEM OF POWER: THE EMERGENCE OF THE MASS-ORIENTED STATE AS THE POLITICAL FORM OF WESTERN CIVILIZATION

In many ways the problem of the state and its authority is the most difficult and permanent with which man has to deal. Despite the confident claims of liberalism, democracy, socialism, fascism, or communism, it seems doubtful that any perfect state—i.e., one that perfectly satisfies all of its citizens—will ever be created. As human circumstances alter, so must the goals and functions of the state, with consequences that are seldom happy for all groups and conditions of men.

In a general way it may be said that the functions of the state depend upon two things: first, whether it exists to serve the welfare of the few or that of the many; and, second, whether it shall be controlled —even when it attempts to serve the interests of most of its citizens— by the few or by the many. For well over a century western man has tended to assume—though there is still some disagreement on the subject—that the state must serve the interests of a majority of its citizens and that they ultimately must have a final control over its decisions. The matter cannot rest, however, on these assumptions and practices of representative democracy, for they are not of themselves sufficient to solve the problems of the state. Even in democratic societies there must remain—and this fact becomes more evident as human problems grow more complex—a distinction between governors and governed between those who actually run the state and make its decisions and those who only approve or disapprove of that which has been done or decided.

Moreover, the state has always been confronted with a seldom resolved dilemma. The act of governing frequently requires an expert knowledge beyond that usually possessed by ordinary men and a willingness on the part of rulers to make decisions that are necessary for the welfare of all but are extremely unpalatable to an important minority or sometimes even a majority of those who compose the political community. Implicit in this dilemma is the problem of power:

1. In whose interests is the power of the state exercised?
2. By whom is the power of the state exercised?

3. Are there limits to the power of the state? What limits, if any, are formed out of ethics? Out of expediency?

By the year 1700 this problem had been temporarily resolved in most western European states with the triumph of the highly centralized absolute monarchy over most other forms of government. England and Holland, however, were two important exceptions. In both of these countries political authority, though far from democratized, was not concentrated in the hands of a king or a royal bureaucracy but was more broadly diffused among the politically significant propertied groups represented in the legislative bodies of those two states. In spite of these exceptions, monarchy was the commonly accepted European form of government and would remain so for more than 200 years. Even in England, where the right of Parliament to limit the king's powers in certain areas had been established by the Glorious Revolution of 1688, the king still wielded very broad powers and possessed an influence that made him a great deal more than a figurehead.

At this point we should remember an important historical fact about monarchical government. For centuries it was not only the most widely accepted but also the most durable European method of rule. Now that it has almost disappeared, we often tend to think of it as having always been arbitrary or unpopular and to assume that those who lived under it were only waiting for an opportune moment to revolt against its authority. Such a belief, while true to some degree of European political attitudes during the last few generations, is not valid as it applies to long periods of earlier history. For the fact is that monarchs and monarchy were not always unpopular. The strong monarchies that came into existence during the fifteenth and sixteenth centuries gave to many European societies a security and stability unknown during the Middle Ages. The king's law and the king's justice, though often imperfectly executed, still provided a greater measure of equality before the law than did feudal courts or customs. The kingly office, too, was a tangible symbol of national power and prestige to an extent seldom achieved by less glamorous elective parliaments or heads of state. But above all else the national monarchies of the early modern period established the practices and patterns of government organization that are still used in democratic states. Modern democracy has retained these while taking over the state and broadening its functions. The state itself, as an institution with clearly defined functions and obligations, was created long before.

Indeed, if we ponder the matter carefully, we can see that without the preparatory spadework of western European kings from the fifteenth through the eighteenth centuries, the modern mass-oriented state could never have come into existence at all. What these kings did over several centuries was to institutionalize their office until it became the vast public corporation we now know as the "state." The process by which they attained this end was often slow and twisted; and they themselves had no clear idea of the goal toward which they were working. If they had, they might have rejected it. In most instances, though they had a vague sense of public responsibility, European kings from the late Middle Ages onward strove toward immediate day-by-day objectives; that is, they were trying to expand their authority at the expense of church and nobles or to convert the uncertain irregular revenues that came to them as feudal overlords of the realm into the regular stipulated payments that we know as taxes. The best evidence of their success may be seen in the gradual transformation of the royal household into a kind of crude state bureaucracy or civil service. At first, most feudal kings were, in theory at least, simply the chief landlords of the realm, though in practice they were more or less than that depending on circumstances and the personal abilities of the individual ruler. As they began slowly to expand their powers, they also necessarily expanded the functions of their personal servants who made up the royal household. Men who had been the king's personal retainers in time found their responsibilities and obligations enlarged as the king extended his authority over feudal society. As the obligations of his servants increased, the king created other offices and institutions to handle the greater volume of royal business. Inevitably, out of this pragmatic growth there developed a body of institutions with their own customs and procedures. Once this stage was reached—and it was attained at different times in different countries—the king no longer ruled his kingdom as a person but as a kind of corporate entity. He had become a symbol of the state.

Even as the national monarchy reached the height of its power during the seventeenth century, however, the very proliferation of its services and obligations created new and more complicated problems. With the growth of wealth and social mobility men were less willing to submit to the complete regulation by the state of all standards, beliefs, or social practices. And while many enjoyed the benefits conferred by strong central authority, they looked upon it with some suspicion and not infrequently resisted its decrees. Furthermore, the property-owning classes often had a strong aversion to meeting the state's demands for the additional revenues needed to keep the state functioning properly. Here we must not forget that most kings did not themselves understand how to resolve this difficulty. Taxation as we know it had not yet come into existence, and most European monarchs, even so late as the seventeenth century, still had to depend on their own private estates for a substantial but often hopelessly inadequate part of the income needed to keep the machinery of government in working order. Nor was there anything like a modern funded or national debt which, by providing for regular repayment of loans made to the state, would have kept the state's credit clean. Most monarchs, therefore, lived a hand-to-mouth existence, always on the verge of bankruptcy and often without money for the most necessary purposes. In their struggle to keep solvent, western European kings were caught in a double squeeze. Not only had the costs of government risen as a result of expanded state functions, but they had also been driven upward by a long process of inflation known as the "price revolution," which had been going on since the sixteenth century. Lacking a modern system of finance, the state staggered from crisis to crisis until some adequate means was found to make up its deficits or, as with England in the seventeenth century and France in the eighteenth century, the disaster of revolution overtook it.

Nevertheless, the new national or absolute monarchy, for all of its difficulties, not only established the pattern of later government but also provided a relatively secure, if not always equable, environment for the expansion of European civilization. In that respect the modern state is another one of the important inventions of western man without which his history would have been very different.

E.   THE DEVELOPMENT OF A GLOBAL SENSE OF HISTORY: EMERGENCE OF THE GREAT REVOLUTIONARY IDEA

By the opening of the eighteenth century literate Europeans and a great many non-Europeans as well had become fully conscious that the world consisted of many diverse peoples and societies other than their own. The discovery had a number of effects, not the least of which for some Europeans was an awareness that their ways of doing things, their traditions, and even their religious beliefs were not superior enough to be accepted immediately by other peoples who came in contact with Europeans. Many of the older traditional societies of Asia, for example, stoutly resisted the incursion of European practices and ideas out of the secure conviction that these were nothing more than the slightly odd cultural manifestations of basically inferior peoples. Many Europeans, impressed by the sophistication of some Asian skills and ways of thought, frequently saw in Chinese or Indian civilization models to be emulated rather than denigrated. The vogue of things Chinese in some western countries during the eighteenth century attests an admiration for what many Europeans thought was a genuinely superior culture with much to teach the West.

As the century advanced, however, more and more non-European peoples were made dependent on Europe by the spread of European world trade and the expansion of European political control over non-European regions. Thus the European sense of cultural and ultimately even ethnic superiority began very slowly to manifest itself in European attitudes toward subject peoples. The rapid expansion of European technological power and industrial wealth heightened the European sense of superiority with a resulting intensification of aggressiveness; this aggression led to the complete absorption of older traditional societies into the governmental system of western imperialism or to the military humiliation of societies that still retained a nominal independence from direct European control.

While this expanded global consciousness was being created by European discovery, conquest, and settlement, there suddenly occurred late in the eighteenth century that great Revolution of the West, whose most important manifestations were to be the American and French revolutions. The impact of those two events reached far beyond their own periods and ultimately transformed humanity's view of history as well as its expectations for the future. Thus the eighteenth century, by giving rise to the massive revolutionary upheaval of the transatlantic world, prepared the way for the far more significant global revolution that would come to pass in the twentieth century.

Index